REGIONALISM IN AMERICAN POLITICS

REGIONALISM IN
AMERICAN
POLITICS

Ira Sharkansky
The University of Wisconsin

The Bobbs-Merrill Company, Inc.
Indianapolis and New York

JAMES A. ROBINSON

The Ohio State University

Consulting Editor in Political Science

Copyright © 1970 by The Bobbs-Merrill Company, Inc.

Printed in the United States of America

Library of Congress Catalog Card Number 69–13635

First Printing

FOR

Stefan and Erica

ACKNOWLEDGMENTS

I have acquired several debts along the way to this book. Professor Delmer D. Dunn read the entire first draft and contributed many helpful suggestions. Andrew T. Cowart helped with many of the details, from data gathering and computing to the organizing of tables. Miss Mary Muessle and Mrs. Elizabeth Landrum did the typing. Three journals—*The Midwest Journal of Political Science,* the *Southwestern Social Science Quarterly,* and the *Western Political Quarterly*—published my early findings about regionalism in politics and public policy. I am indebted to *The Western Political Quarterly* for permission to incorporate portions of my article, "Regional Patterns in the Expenditures of American States," XX (December 1967), 955–971. Financial support came from the Committee on Governmental and Legal Processes of the Social Science Research Council, and the Office of General Research of the University of Georgia. And through it all, my wife Ina earned all of the thanks that is customarily paid to a spouse.

I.S.

May 1968

CONTENTS

LIST OF TABLES

LIST OF MAPS

REGIONALISM IN AMERICAN POLITICS

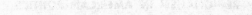

1

INTRODUCTION

This book is about regional peculiarities in politics and public policies—peculiarities which reflect a number of social, economic, and political processes that have had similar effects upon neighboring states. In several parts of the country, the first white settlers came from a common stream of migration; their values and attitudes left an imprint on the structure and policies of early state governments, and are still apparent in the present character of politics and government programs. Similar kinds of natural resources, or opportunities for the development of industry, have given neighboring states common economic experiences. In the South, the common factors of war, reconstruction, racial heterogeneity, and continuing poverty have molded a distinctive approach to political participation and competition and to the provision of public services. Such factors have made regional norms important for the officials of most states; and these norms are, in turn, reinforced by the consulting patterns of contemporary officials, who know their counterparts in nearby states and feel that their neighbors face problems that are similar to their own. Thus, they are most likely to consult with regional partners when they plan new activities.

There is, of course, diversity within regions, as well. The inhabitants of the mountain countries from western Virginia in the north through Tennessee, the western Carolinas, north Georgia, and northern Alabama show attitudes toward the Civil War and the Republican party that are greatly at odds with those of lowlanders in the same states. In the Middle-Western region, Ohio, Missouri, Indiana, and Illinois—all of which received early settlers from both the Northeast and the upper Southern states—continue to show contrasting political patterns within themselves that reflect the residue from those early settlements.

Yet the distinctiveness of regions is more to the point of this book than are intra-regional variations. Some of the sharpest differences in public affairs can be found in comparisons of politics from one section of the country to another, and several regional oddities have long been the subject of unsystematic political observation. In many communities of the Northeast, for example, the national origin of a candidate's grandfather appears to be an important item of public information. Politics in the South is often marked by undecipherable combinations of candidates and supporters in transient factions of the Democratic party; the regional heritage of Southern politicians is further reflected in their frequent public support of the Bible and their attacks on alcohol and federal intervention. Policy needs, too, differ markedly among regions. Politics in the West revolves about grass, water, mineral exploitation, and the need to facilitate transportation across still-wide-open spaces. On the other hand, policy planners in Eastern states must somehow deal with the effluvia of population concentration. It is apparent that Southern states rank lowest on most measures of payments to welfare recipients; that New Englanders pay more property tax per capita than the residents of most other regions; that local governments in the Great Lakes states carry the heaviest burdens of financing public services; and that state and local governments in the Far West spend the most money per capita. These traits are not merely the curious remnants of regional histories. They reveal that regionalism is still viable in American politics: it leaves an imprint on the character of political campaigns and the nature of services that citizens receive from their governments.

Regionalism and Comparative State Politics

Although regionalism is emphasized in the title of this book and in the substance of most chapters, we shall also concern ourselves with one other major topic: the comparative analysis of state politics and public policies. Actually, this book stands at the confluence of two bodies of literature. The first focuses upon regional patterns of politics; it includes the work of sociologists, economists, planners, and political scientists who advocate the use of regions in the planning and administration of national programs, and that of political scientists who describe the activities of citizens, politicians, and government agencies in individual regions. The second body of literature, more recently developed, consists of those studies which have used the American states as a laboratory of comparative analysis. By means of "hard" data and sophisticated statistical techniques, its contributors have tried to identify the social, economic, and political features associated with various patterns in state politics and policy: the level of "economic development" in each state, the incidence of popular participation in politics, the degree of two-party competition, the equity of urban-rural apportionment in the state legislatures, and the level of "professionalism" in those legislatures. It is not accurate to imply that only the second body of literature employs techniques of comparative analysis. Some of the regional studies explicitly compare different states, but there is generally nothing more than intra-regional analysis: the states of different regions are rarely compared. Because of this narrow scope, most of the regional literature suffers from lack of a clear understanding about how each region stands in relation to the larger political context.

Both the literature of "regionalism" and that of "comparative state politics" show certain deficiencies that we hope to remedy in this book. The major problems in the regional literature are:

1. A failure to compare the region at issue with other regions, or with the remainder of the country, leading to some questionable conclusions about the distinctiveness of politics in that region.

2. A failure to consider alternate definitions of the region. To focus on one combination of states, labeling them "South," "West," "Midwest," etc., is to beg the question of which states should be included, and which excluded, from the region. Without testing for the political characteristics of several combinations of core and peripheral states, it is not possible to conclude with certainty about the politics or policies of "a region."

3. A failure to test for likely economic or social determinants of findings which may create the appearance of distinctive political traits in a region. The level of a state's economic development obviously has something to do with the nature of its politics or policies; it is risky to talk about the political determinants of a regional pattern without first ascertaining that the pattern does not merely reflect the level of economic development in the region.

4. A failure to explore a wide range of political and policy factors on a regional basis. Most of the regional literature deals with manifestations of voter participation in state politics, the intensity of two-party competition, or the style of elected officials. There are few systematic intra- and interregional comparisons of the equity of legislative apportionment, the degree of "professionalism" and "activism" in the state legislature and state bureaucracies, the nature of state and local government revenue systems, intergovernmental financial relationships, and levels of government spending and performance in the major fields of service.

This book attempts to correct for these shortcomings in the regional literature. First, it considers regions throughout the 48 contiguous states (omitting Alaska and Hawaii on the assumption that regions reflect shared historical experiences among neighboring states, whereas the historical experiences of Alaska and Hawaii have been fairly isolated and neither state has any immediate neighbors). Second, this book departs from the established pattern by considering multiple definitions of American regions. Instead of using one definition each for the major regions, subsequent chapters work with 17 regional groupings of the states; Delaware, for example, is tested for its regional similarities not only to the South and the Border states, but also to those of the North and Middle Atlantic. These groupings will be discussed in the next chapter; we will merely list them here:

North	Upper Middle West	Southwest
Northeast	Plains	Transplains
New England	South	Transmississippi
Mid-Atlantic	Southeast	Mountains
Great Lakes	Confederacy	Far West
Northcentral	Border States	

Third, this book employs systematic tests so that regional traits of politics and public policies which merely reflect current economic characteristics shared by neighboring states can be distinguished from those traits that reflect more deeply ingrained regional patterns. We shall apply historical, cultural, or political explanations only to those regional characteristics that we cannot explain more simply by reference to current economic conditions. Finally, this book differs from its predecessors in the content of politics that it investigates. Although it does deal with the electoral processes and party phenomena that are the topics of existing literature, it also considers several other political characteristics and the nature of major public services in each region. Thus, the relationships between state and local governments, the nature of urban-rural apportionment in state legislatures, the professionalism of state legislatures, government expenditures, financial relationships of federal, state, and local governments, government indebtedness, tax structures, the nature of state and local bureaucracies, and levels of public service in the major fields of education, highways, and public welfare are all considered in a regional framework.

The major problems in the existing literature of comparative state politics, on the other hand, are as follows:

1. A limited conception of factors considered in the analysis of state politics. This literature has often made sweeping claims about the role of "the political system" as an influence on policy, but those claims are based upon a limited assessment of inter-party competition, voter turnout, and the equity of legislative apportionment. Such studies of "politics" neglect measurements pertaining to interest groups, the nature of party organizations, the styles of candidates and elected officials, the characteristics of state legislators and government employees, the nature of criteria taken into consideration by policy makers in state and local government agencies, the role of the press, nationality groups, and religious leaders in state politics, and relationships between federal, state, and local units of government.

2. A concentration on the gross findings that come from the aggregate analysis of 48 or fifty states. Although some contributors to this literature have made some analyses of the "South" apart from other states, there is generally no awareness that findings produced by a fifty-state analysis may differ considerably from what exists in the environments of different regions.

3. A fixation on analyses made at a single point in time. The few studies that do consider the time dimension reveal that the relationships between comparable factors differ sharply at earlier and later periods. Some studies have found, moreover, that officials' assessments of their own decisions in the past are critical ingredients of their current decisions. Consequently, investigations that fail to consider the past run the severe risk of developing elaborate theoretical justifications for empirical findings that may have only transient relevance.

This book will add to the literature of comparative state politics by considering "region" as a nominal variable that may help to explain interstate differences in politics and public policy. "Region" will be compared with "economic development" as likely determinants of politics and policy. Although "region" shows great statistical weight with respect to measures of politics and policy, "region" by itself is a poorly contrived explanation. One of our principal tasks, then, will be to suggest historical, cultural, and behavioral explanations for our regional findings.

In order to assess regional patterns in politics and public policy, we shall identify those regions in which the level of economic development is a more or less satisfactory explanation of each characteristic. We shall inquire, for example, whether the states below the Ohio River show the traits of one-party politics, limited participation in politics, and low levels of education and welfare services simply because they are poor, or because of other features that are associated with their *southernness*. Where the level of economic development does not provide a satisfactory explanation for our findings, we shall suggest other characteristics of the regions that appear to be relevant.

As part of our inquiry into regional patterns of politics and policy, we shall make some longitudinal analyses that go back to 1902. With this data we can explore the hypothesis that American politics are becoming homogenized under the influence of federal grants, population mobility, and improved nationwide transportation and communication. Our findings reveal the continued—and in several cases increased—vitality of regional patterns, and point to several elements which seem important in maintaining these patterns.

Before the reader embarks on our undertaking of description and analysis, he may wish to review the two bodies of literature that have prepared the way for this study; he will then be able to appreciate how the ideas employed in this book relate to those that have been used previously in the social sciences. In deference to those who wish to proceed without this review, however, we have placed it in Appendix A.

Regionalism in the Attitudes and Behaviors of State Elites

A basic assumption in this book is that regional similarities in state politics and public policy reflect some underlying behavioral processes whereby the structure and outputs of politics in neighboring states come to resemble one another. For the most part, this assumption will have to rest on itself, for there is little solid evidence about the political intercourse between the elites of different states. However, the results of one study made in the South indicate (although the evidence is fragmentary) that decision makers in state governments do consult with their neighbors about new issues in public policy. As part of a survey among the budget officers of 67 major agencies [1] in the states of Florida, Georgia, Kentucky, and Mississippi, an attempt was made to identify the states that served as the budgeteers' reference group. One question was: "Have you or any of your colleagues contacted officials in other states in any attempt to learn how they deal with a particular situation that you have encountered in your work?" Where a budget officer answered in the affirmative, he was asked: "What states do you feel are the best sources of information?" The 67 respondents made 198 nominations of such states; most (87 percent) of their nominations were in the region composed of the eleven states of the Confederacy and the Border states of Delaware, Maryland, Kentucky, West Virginia, and Oklahoma, and 35 percent of the states nominated bordered directly on those of the respondents. It is conceivable that Southerners are more parochial in their perceptions of reference-states than officials in other sections of the country; yet officials elsewhere (questioned informally about their reference-states during interviews) likewise referred primarily to states that are immediate or near neighbors.

A similar survey conducted among school superintendents within the state of Georgia provided some insight into the regional orientation of local government officers. A sample of twenty superintendents, asked who they contacted when they felt the need to discuss a local problem with an outside expert, showed a strong tendency to communicate with other superintendents who were immediate neighbors, or partners in an administrative region of the state. In Georgia, these regions are coterminous with the Congressional Districts. The superintendents in each district have periodic meetings, and they come to know their counterparts throughout the district.

[1] A major agency was defined as one having a budget of at least one million dollars during the year of the survey (1966).

The school superintendents gave a total of 36 nominations when they were asked to identify the outside persons with whom they communicated most frequently. Forty-two percent of those nominated were fellow superintendents in contiguous districts, 56 percent were within the Congressional District, and 70 percent were either contiguous, within the Congressional District, or within a common metropolitan area. The statements of the superintendents suggest that their choice of contacts is an uncomplicated one, guided by a notion of friends and neighbors within easy reach. One superintendent in a rural district lives several miles from his place of work, and described his daily drive as the guide to his contacts: "Well, I live in Macon County, so I have to drive through Marion and Schley Counties. I talk with those three pretty often." Several of the superintendents in the survey administered relatively large, urban districts. But only one of these —the superintendent in Chatham County (Savannah), who mentioned superintendents in other large Georgia cities—differed from the prevailing regional orientation in selecting his contacts.

Although it seems clear that government officials are inclined to look within their region for policy cues, the question remains: Which regional partners are usually the subject of emulation? The comments of several officials suggest that the governments which have acquired a reputation for leadership in a certain service field are sought out disproportionately for their advice. Professor Jack L. Walker of the University of Michigan has gathered evidence on the timing of innovations in each of the 48 contiguous states. By aggregating evidence across several fields of service he has ranked the states according to their tendency to adopt programs or policies earlier than other states. His rankings (repeated in Table 1–1) indicate that New York and Massachusetts play leadership roles in the Northeast, Michigan and Wisconsin in the middle section of the country, California on the West Coast, Colorado in the Mountain region and Louisiana and Virginia in the South.[2] Officials of leading states within each region seem more likely

2 Jack L. Walker, "The Adoption of Innovations by the American States," a paper delivered at the Annual Meeting of the American Political Science Association, Washington, 1968. Mimeo.

TABLE 1-1. RANKINGS OF THE STATES ON A COMPOSITE INDEX OF PROGRAM INNOVATION

1. New York	17. New Hampshire	33. Idaho
2. Massachusetts	18. Indiana	34. Tennessee
3. California	19. Louisiana	35. West Virginia
4. New Jersey	20. Maine	36. Arizona
5. Michigan	21. Virginia	37. Georgia
6. Connecticut	22. Utah	38. Montana
7. Pennsylvania	23. North Dakota	39. Missouri
8. Oregon	24. North Carolina	40. Delaware
9. Colorado	25. Kansas	41. New Mexico
10. Wisconsin	26. Nebraska	42. Oklahoma
11. Ohio	27. Kentucky	43. South Dakota
12. Minnesota	28. Vermont	44. Texas
13. Illinois	29. Iowa	45. South Carolina
14. Washington	30. Alabama	46. Wyoming
15. Rhode Island	31. Florida	47. Nevada
16. Maryland	32. Arkansas	48. Mississippi

From Jack L. Walker, "The Adoption of Innovations by the American States," paper delivered at the 1968 Annual Meeting of the American Political Science Association. Reprinted by permission of Jack L. Walker.

to generate their own innovations, or take their cues from national leaders. This follow-the-regional-leader communications network helps to isolate most states from direct national influences, and permits the development of regional approaches to new programs—even when such programs are sponsored and "regulated" by federal agencies.

Features Supporting the Regional Orientation of Public Officials

The tendency of political leaders and government officials to acquire their cues from regional neighbors has several causes: the belief that neighbors have problems similar to one's own; the attitude among officials and interested citizens that it is "legitimate" to adapt one's programs to those of nearby governments; and the structure of officials' organizational affiliations, which put them into frequent contact with counterparts in neighboring governments.

The belief that officials of neighboring jurisdictions have similar problems is expressed in simple fashion by public officials; beneath it, however, lies a complex set of reasons. On the surface, it means that elites in neighboring states probably have encountered policy questions similar to those currently being faced; consequently the neighbor is likely to have a concrete suggestion to offer or to be informed about the pitfalls to be encountered along the way to certain solutions. But underlying this expectation is the more basic assumption: that the neighboring government is serving a population akin to one's own, with similar needs for public service and similar demands on government agencies. The neighboring government's economy is likely to be similar, presenting a comparable set of resources and needs to government agencies; the same resemblance usually exists between the political environments, with respect to the levels of service that can receive popular support and to the relationships among administrators, executives, legislators, and private interests.

Such resemblances in the population and the economic and political characteristics of neighboring jurisdictions may result from underlying geographical similarities, leading to similar economic and population characteristics; or from shared historical experiences, which may give rise to common political values and similar desires for public services. The state governments in the South, which are commonly perceived to represent the archetype of American regions, share certain geographical features that have influenced politics through the intermediary of the cotton–plantation–slave–race syndrome. And their shared historical experiences of racial heterogeneity, the Civil War and Reconstruction, continuing poverty, limited political participation, and limited competition seem to have left their imprint on current features of public service.

Because one's neighbors face similar problems with similar resources, the norms which guide their own service decisions are likely to be within reach of one's own agency; thus, the adaptation to regional models is considered "relevant," "easy," or "feasible" in the light of local conditions. For officials in the state of Georgia, it would be reasonable (that is, legitimate) to adopt patterns found in Florida, North Carolina, or Tennessee, while those found in New York, Michigan, or California have been considered "out of reach," "impractical," or "designed for a different set of needs."

Regional comparisons also draw their legitimacy from the past experience of politicians, journalists, and members of the public who take an interest in certain programs, and who usually compare efforts within their native state to those in their own circle of experience—a circle that is typically limited to the region. Moreover, state bureaus of research usually publish comparisons of their own state's demographic, economic, and public-service characteristics with those of regional partners. This information provides additional fuel and status to the comparison of one's own efforts with those of the neighborhood. In the *Georgia Statistical Abstract,* for example (published by the University's Bureau of Business and Economic Research), data for Georgia are compared with a figure for the entire United States, and with separate figures for Alabama, Florida, North Carolina, South Carolina, and Tennessee; and *Wisconsin's State and Local Tax Burden,* a policy analysis prepared by a study committee of the University of Wisconsin, compares the data for Wisconsin with that for Illinois, Indiana, Iowa, Michigan, Minnesota, and Ohio. Many regionally oriented public officials have a sense for interstate competition that inclines them to services no lower and taxes no higher than regional norms.

The legitimacy of regional comparisons tends to feed upon its own past habit. Officials have learned which of their counterparts in nearby governments will supply credible information, and which have good judgment. Unless an official is committed to an extensive program of research before making his own policy decision, he may be satisfied with the guidance received as the result of a few calls placed to individuals with whom he has dealt amicably in the past.

The organizational experiences of government officials, as well, incline them to take their policy cues from regional neighbors. State and local government personnel often belong to formal national organizations, according to their subject-matter specialty. There were 46 of these groups in 1966,[3] including such units as the National Association of State Budget Officers, the National Association of State Conservation Officers, and the National Association of Housing and Redevelopment Officials. These organizations have both national and regional divisions. Their periodic meetings are a means for trading information about current problems, and they reinforce acquaintanceships formed at earlier meetings. State and local officials indicate that they are more likely to attend the regional meetings of these groups than the national ones, and that many of their outside contacts are first acquired at these meetings.

The federal government agencies that distribute grants-in-aid to state and local units helped to establish some of these associations, regarding them as informal communications media which would supplement the formal communications between granting and receiving agencies. Certain grants authorize the use of federal funds for the dues of state agency memberships in these organizations, so that the federal government provides a continuing subsidy to keep them in operation. The regional offices of federal agencies also encourage intra-regional communications; the cities of New York, Atlanta, Chicago, Dallas, Kansas City, Denver, and San Francisco have acquired informal status as regional capitals because they contain numerous field offices of Washington agencies. The personnel in these field offices conduct most of the correspondence between the federal agency and state and local units, and pass news about problems and solutions from one state government to the next within their regions. In several ways, federal agencies have reinforced the regional orientations among state and local officials. These orientations have subsequently produced regional variants of several federally sponsored programs.

Except for the argument that state politics and public policies show significant regional differences, this book does not set

3 *Ibid.*

out to test a specific thesis. Its more important task is to seek answers for the following questions:

1. How do the state politics and public policies of each region differ?

2. How consistent are the patterns within each region —that is, what diversities in politics and public policies exist within each region?

3. To what extent do regional traits in politics and policies merely reflect the regional distribution of economic resources among the states?

4. For those regional differences in politics and policies that cannot be traced to current economic characteristics, what other experiences shared by neighboring states provide an explanation for the regional peculiarities?

Chapter 2 lays the ground rules to be used in answering these questions; it defines 17 regions that are employed in our study, lists the political variables that will be subject to analysis, and describes the statistical techniques to be used. Chapter 3 defines regional differences in several measures of politics and public policies, and examines the consistency of each trait within each region. Chapter 4 examines changes in the distinctiveness of regional traits during the twentieth century. Chapter 5 discusses the relationships among economics, politics, and public policies, and assesses the relative influence upon politics and public policies of current economic characteristics and regional characteristics independent of current economics. Chapter 6 speculates about some experiences that account for the regional peculiarities which are not explained by current economic characteristics; and finally, Chapter 7 looks at the case of state government expenditures in an effort to determine if links among principal features in the policy-making process differ from one region to the next.

2

THE EMPIRICAL ANALYSIS
OF REGIONS

It is the task of this chapter to describe the groupings of states that are employed here, and to specify the analytical procedure that will be followed. As is noted in Chapter 1, the scheme employed in mapping the regions of America might bias the findings of our research. Likewise, the components of politics and public policy considered may influence our view of regional peculiarities. In order to minimize the distortions that may result from limited conceptions of "regions," "politics," or "policy," we shall employ multiple definitions of our principal variables.

This chapter defines 17 regional groupings of the states and 61 measures of politics and policy that will provide the focus of our research, and explains the statistical tests that will permit us to simplify the mass of findings produced by these combinations of regions and traits. The tests will indicate the specific regions that are most distinctive politically, and the relative importance of current economic characteristics in producing the regional patterns that appear.

The regions to be described include several groupings that are widely documented in other studies of history and public affairs. We find New England, the South, and the Far West, but also some regions that comprise odd configurations of states under unusual labels: Transplains, Upper Middle West, and Transmississippi. It is obvious that 17 groupings of the American states cannot be arrived at without considerable prior analysis. The boundaries of almost all of our regions mask some debatable assumptions about the most appropriate groups of states. Because of the controversies inherent in the process of selection, it is necessary to explain the reasons for considering each group as a region.

Three methodological issues lie at the heart of the regional choices that are made: (1) the issue of a single or multiple demarcations of the United States; (2) the issue of border states; and (3) the issue of contiguity within regions. Stated in different terms, the first issue concerns the need for so many regions. Why devise 17 when the most prominent political science literature has limited its concern to a mere six: New England, South, Middle West, West, Rocky Mountains, and Border States? The second issue is related to the first, and it helps to explain the need to consider many regional demarcations. Briefly stated, the issue of border states arises because reasonable observers have great difficulty in selecting the boundaries of each region. For each demarcation there are good reasons for adding or subtracting one or more states from the first-suggested geographical outline. Because a single division of the national pie is not satisfactory, we use many pies and divide each in a different way. The third issue concerns the need to maintain contiguity among the states of each region. Can a region exist when several states seem to share politically relevant traits, even though the states are separated by other states that do not share their regional affiliation? Although it is clear that widely separated states may share politically relevant traits (Vermont and West Virginia or Florida and Arizona are two pairs that provide examples), this book will insist that there be some ties of geography among regional partners. For reasons that should become apparent to the reader, the "region" as an explanatory concept in political science is already an imprecise independent variable whose strength lies in its association with the historical experiences and contemporary characteristics shared by neighboring states and the tendency of state elites to consult with their counterparts in neighboring states. If we discard the component of contiguity, "region" may lose much of its existing meaning.

States as Units for Regional Analysis

Before we face any of these issues, however, it is necessary to resolve one basic question: Are the states meaningful units of analysis for an inquiry into American regionalism? Our entire undertaking is built upon data that reflect conditions on a statewide basis, yet it is evident that the borders of the states make imperfect regional boundaries. Some important regions cut through several states without including the entirety of any of them, and the boundaries between distinct geographical or cultural areas frequently bisect several states and do not cleanly coincide with the borders between any two states. In the South, the black belt of high nonwhite concentration and productive agriculture cuts a swath from Texas to Virginia, but shows political characteristics significantly different from those in other sections of these states. The black belt contrasts most sharply with another intra-southern region, the Appalachian, which extends from northern Alabama and Georgia to western Virginia. In the Northeast, the heavily populated, Catholic, industrialized coastal sections exhibit a style of politics that differs from that in the rural, Protestant interior. In the Middle West, contrasting streams of migration brought Southerners and New Englanders into different sections of Ohio, Indiana, and Illinois. The residue of these settlements still shows itself in the party alignments of entire communities. And in the West, the terrain, economy, and requirements for public services shift from plains to mountains at a boundary that cuts through the states of Montana, Wyoming, and Colorado.

Few states, then, may actually be termed homogeneous in their culture, economy or politics. Howard W. Odum and Harry E. Moore recognized this thirty years ago in their major work on American regionalism: "Most states contain more than one economic and social region; most regions contain more than one state." [1] However, the states remain useful as

---

[1] Howard W. Odum and Harry E. Moore, *American Regionalism* (New York: Henry Holt, 1938), p. 383.

the building-blocks of our regions. There is a wealth of data available on the social, economic, and political characteristics of each state, and much of it is available *only* on a state-by-state basis. Moreover, the states do have a political reality, and they are producers of public policy. State governments have political functions that are not possessed by intra-state or multi-state regions. They make policies for their own implementation and they regulate the policy-making activities of local governments within their borders. Insofar as the policies of state and local governments are among the topics we are considering on a regional basis, it is necessary to have the states as our integral units. Odum and Moore summed up the case for using groups of entire states as regions:

> All of these considerations and others lead to the conclusion, therefore, that the group-of-states major region(s) will qualify best as the composite region(s) which approximates the largest number and variety of indices available for the largest number of purposes or classifications. . . . it would seem that the natural region, no matter what specialized advantages it offers, cannot qualify as the key major region not only because it cannot be made to coincide with the societal or cultural region, but because it is not practically realistic. Range of climate, topography, historical and cultural diversity militate against its use as a composite cultural region. Such regions do not, therefore, approximate adequacy without ignoring the legal, sovereign, cultural foundations of the nation. More important, however, as the irreducible criterion of reality is the historical, constitutional, and organizational status of the 48 states, which are the very warp and woof of our national fabric.[2]

The Issue of Single or Multiple Demarcations

In each of the existing books about regional politics the authors employ a single definition of their subject, and fail to compare it with other regions. The South of V. O. Key's *South-*

2 *Ibid.,* p. 33.

ern Politics: In State and Nation includes the eleven states of the Confederacy: Virginia, North Carolina, South Carolina, Georgia, Florida, Tennessee, Alabama, Mississippi, Louisiana, Arkansas, and Texas.[3] The states considered in John H. Fenton's *Politics in the Border States* are Maryland, Kentucky, West Virginia, and Missouri; [4] in his *Midwest Politics,* Fenton examines Ohio, Indiana, Illinois, Michigan, Wisconsin, and Minnesota.[5] In *Rocky Mountain Politics,* Thomas C. Donnelly includes articles about Montana, Wyoming, Colorado, New Mexico, Idaho, Utah, Arizona, and Nevada.[6] When Frank H. Jonas edited *Western Politics* along Donnelly's model twenty years later, he added to these states California, Oregon, Washington, Alaska, and Hawaii.[7] As expected, Duane Lockard's *New England State Politics* covers the six states east of the Hudson River.[8]

Depending upon the authors' intentions, the focus on a single definition of any region can be merely annoying or methodologically suspect. If an author intends to describe the politics of certain states that are contiguous, then the reader may only be annoyed at not having further discussions of nearby states that might qualify as members of the region. The edited collections by Donnelly and Jonas come closest to simple descriptions of state politics within their regions: each state is the subject of a separate chapter composed by a political scientist who has some knowledge of the state, and there is only a minimal attempt to weave the separate chapters into an integrated discussion of the region. Yet even in these volumes there are claims about the distinctiveness of the Rocky Mountain area or the West that a reader cannot test without an

[3] V. O. Key, *Southern Politics: In State and Nation* (New York: Alfred A. Knopf, 1949).

[4] John H. Fenton, *Politics in the Border States* (New Orleans: The Hauser Press, 1957).

[5] John H. Fenton, *Midwest Politics* (New York: Holt, Rinehart and Winston, 1966).

[6] Thomas C. Donnelly, *Rocky Mountain Politics* (Albuquerque: University of New Mexico Press, 1940).

[7] Frank H. Jonas, *Western Politics* (Salt Lake City: University of Utah Press, 1961).

[8] Duane Lockard, *New England State Politics* (Princeton: Princeton University Press, 1959).

opportunity to determine if politics in the bordering states are significantly different from those within the authors' conception of the region.

Where the author makes explicit statements about the distinctiveness of a region, his concentration upon a single geographical definition precludes the readers' acceptance of his claims. Duane Lockard writes that he is studying the politics of New England states so that he can test certain propositions, such as the impact of party competition on the policies of state governments, in a context of similar political heritage, governmental structure and social-economic characteristics. However, he leaves his reader wondering about his choice of a laboratory. Although the borders of "New England" are clear, they do not enclose a homogeneous governmental, social, or economic entity. The northern states of that region differ from their southern neighbors in social-economic characteristics as well as in the nature of two-party competition. Lockard wrote about the consistent differences between northern and southern New England in levels of party competition and the generosity of public services, but it is possible that these may stem from intra-regional differences on economic characteristics rather than party competition.[9] If Lockard wished to study politics in similar social and economic environments, then a grouping of southern New England with New York, New Jersey, and Pennsylvania would be more desirable than all of New England alone.

John Fenton's choice of four Border states in which to examine politics as they are likely to become in the Deep South is even more suspect than Lockard's focus on New England. Fenton omitted Delaware and Oklahoma, states that are frequently grouped in this region along with Maryland, West Virginia, Kentucky, and Missouri on the usual definition of the Border states as those on the fringes of the Old South that share important economic, social, or political traits of the South. Delaware was a slave state and included active secessionist elements during the Civil War; Oklahoma was settled partly by Southerners who carried their notions about racial separation with them into the new territory. Both, along with

9 Richard E. Dawson and James A. Robinson, "Interparty Competition, Economic Variables, and Welfare Politics in the American States," *Journal of Politics*, XXV (May 1963), 264–289.

the other Border and Southern states, required segregated public schools until the 1954 Supreme Court decision. Fenton does not explain his exclusion of Oklahoma and Delaware from his region; as a result a reader cannot determine if his findings would be strengthened or diluted by the consideration of the other states that are commonly considered to be regional partners. In his *Midwest Politics* Fenton similarly fails to explain his focus on an abbreviated region. He finds consistent differences between the characteristics of political parties in Ohio, Indiana, and Illinois, and in Michigan, Wisconsin, and Minnesota; he attributes these differences to the peculiar historical experiences of the northern and southern "Middle West." Although Fenton's argument makes some sense in the light of the states he examines, a reader is disturbed at the exclusion of other states that are usually grouped in the Middle West: Iowa, Missouri, the Dakotas, Nebraska, and Kansas. Each of these states shares certain elements of political and economic background with the states that Fenton examines, but the reader cannot determine if his propositions work in the larger region.

A principal advantage for the multiple definitions of regions is the insight it provides into the uniformities within greater sections of the country. By considering a large regional definition for the Northeast alongside of the findings for New England or the Middle Atlantic, for example, it is possible to determine the analytic utility of dividing the Northeast. And because the analysis also examines regional groupings in other sections of the nation, it is possible to identify with some certainty the salient borders of the Northeast. Much of the justification for the multiple definition of regions is identical with the precept that requires the use of multiple indicators in any scientific inquiry: *in the absence of clearly defined abstractions whose ingredients are widely accepted by experts, it is necessary to test one's findings with a variety of measurements that make different assessments of the subject at hand.*[10] Because many experts among academicians do not accept single definitions of American regions, it is necessary to con-

[10] Eugene J. Webb, Donald T. Campbell, Richard D. Schwartz, and Lee Sechrest, *Unobtrusive Measures: Nonreactive Research in the Social Sciences* (Chicago: Rand McNally, 1966).

vince them of one's findings by making one's demonstration with a number of regional demarcations. Only New England has widely accepted regional borders; and although social scientists agree on the definition of New England as the six states east of the Hudson River, they do not agree that New England is a significant region for purposes of political analysis. To demonstrate the distinctiveness of New England, it is necessary to compare its traits to those of various combinations of nearby states (such as the Middle Atlantic and the larger Northeast) that may resemble the New England states as closely as each of the New England states resembles one another.

When an author fails to make a systematic comparison between his region and others, it is not possible to accept any claim that his region is peculiar. While most observers would agree that politics differ between the Northeast, South, and West, the specific nature of regional differences cannot appear in the examination of one region alone. Only by looking more broadly at the nation is it possible to identify the regions that show uniform and distinctive traits, and to determine the analytic utility of the region as an ordering concept in political science. As a result of the nationwide focus of this volume, it will be possible to show that New England and the states of the Old Confederacy *do not* demonstrate intra-regional uniformity on all dimensions of politics. On several important characteristics the states of Vermont and Mississippi resemble one another more closely than each resembles its regional neighbors.

The Issue of Border States

At its heart, the problem of a single definition for each region is a problem of border states: just where does one region blend off to meet another region? Daniel J. Elazar has argued cogently that regional borders are within states rather than between states,[11] but the nature of the data used in this book requires that state boundaries be used as regional boundaries. Because individual border states may show in their

[11] Daniel J. Elazar, *American Federalism: A View From the States* (New York: Thomas Y. Crowell, 1966).

own political characteristics certain traits that align them with each of two (or more) regions, the problem is actually multiple, involving the identification of likely borders between regions; and where these borders go through states rather than between them, it is necessary to be Solomon-like in assigning each border state to the region that it reflects most completely. Fortunately the Solomon analogy is not perfect. While the Biblical king could not produce additional babies to pacify the two contending "mothers," we can devise additional regional demarcations and try out each problematical border state in as many regions as there are contenders. Out of this resolution of the border state problem comes another pragmatic justification for the multiple demarcation of regions: where experts do not agree on the regional assignments of individual border states, it is possible to create enough regions to test most claims.

The Issue of Contiguity

Because it is shared traits that make the politics of regional neighbors distinctive, it is tempting to inquire about the importance of contiguity for "regionalism." An analyst focusing on politically relevant characteristics of the states might group various states into "regions" without regard to their proximity. Thus, Delaware, Connecticut, and Nevada might be examined for political similarities that grow out of the combined traits of small population and high average personal income, or states from the Rocky Mountains and southern New England areas might be grouped for the purpose of examining their common traits of high voter turnout and intense two-party competition.

It is true that a nationwide analysis of the states' economic and political characteristics will produce some meaningful insights into the political process; there is a large and growing literature (reviewed in Appendix A) which examines economic, social, and political traits that cluster together in the states and help to explain one another. It seems unwise, however, to confuse comparative state analysis with a regional inquiry. At the heart of the regional analysis is the assumption that traits shared by neighboring states reflect shared historical experiences and the tendency of neighbors to consult among themselves. A regional analysis is a form of comparative state inquiry, but its distinctiveness should be maintained by insisting on contiguity.

The Regions of America

The preceding discussion should make it evident that the regions considered in this book cover the whole of the conti-

TABLE 2–1. THE REGIONS AND THEIR MEMBER STATES

Northern and Eastern

NORTH	NORTHEAST	Rhode Island
Maine	Maine	Connecticut
New Hampshire	New Hampshire	
Vermont	Vermont	MIDDLE ATLANTIC
Massachusetts	Massachusetts	New York
Rhode Island	Rhode Island	New Jersey
Connecticut	Connecticut	Pennsylvania
New York	New York	Delaware
New Jersey	New Jersey	Maryland
Pennsylvania	Pennsylvania	
Delaware		GREAT LAKES
Maryland	NEW ENGLAND	
Ohio		Ohio
Indiana	Maine	Indiana
Michigan	New Hampshire	Michigan
Illinois	Vermont	Illinois
Wisconsin	Massachusetts	Wisconsin

Northern and Central

NORTHCENTRAL	North Dakota	PLAINS
Ohio	South Dakota	Minnesota
Indiana	Nebraska	Iowa
Michigan	Kansas	Missouri
Illinois		North Dakota
Wisconsin	UPPER MIDDLE WEST	South Dakota
Minnesota	Michigan	Nebraska
Iowa	Wisconsin	Kansas
Missouri	Minnesota	
	North Dakota	

TABLE 2–1 (Continued)

Southern

SOUTH
Delaware
Maryland
Virginia
West Virginia
North Carolina
South Carolina
Georgia
Florida
Kentucky
Tennessee
Alabama
Mississippi
Arkansas
Louisiana
Oklahoma
Texas

BORDER STATES
Delaware
Maryland
West Virginia
Kentucky
Missouri
Oklahoma

CONFEDERACY
Virginia
North Carolina
South Carolina
Georgia
Florida
Tennessee
Alabama
Mississippi

Arkansas
Louisiana
Texas

SOUTHEAST
Virginia
West Virginia
North Carolina
South Carolina
Georgia
Florida
Kentucky
Tennessee
Alabama
Mississippi
Arkansas
Louisiana

Western

TRANSMISSISSIPPI
Minnesota
Iowa
Missouri
North Dakota
South Dakota
Nebraska
Kansas
Oklahoma
Texas
Montana
Wyoming
Colorado
New Mexico
Idaho
Utah
Arizona

Washington
Oregon
Nevada
California

TRANSPLAINS
Montana
Wyoming
Colorado
New Mexico
Idaho
Utah
Arizona
Washington
Oregon
Nevada
California

MOUNTAINS
Montana
Wyoming
Colorado
Idaho
Utah

SOUTHWEST
Oklahoma
Texas
New Mexico
Arizona

FAR WEST
Washington
Oregon
Nevada
California

nental United States; that each state is placed in several different combinations with its neighbors; and that the principle of contiguity is honored in the demarcations. However, these guidelines are minimum conditions, and do not indicate the regions that are considered. Our regions bring together 17 groups of states that show certain similarities in politics and public policies. Table 2–1 lists the member states in each region.

Admittedly, some element of arbitrary selection has entered into the choice of regions. Although an effort was made to include each of the regions that has been considered salient in the literature of American politics, the total number was held down for the sake of simplicity and clarity of presentation. Undoubtedly the choices that were made will offend some area specialists who perceive that a slightly different grouping of the states would shed important light on our findings.

Of the 17 regions that will be considered in this book, 14 are found in three demarcations of the 48 states that have been widely used by economists, demographers, and political scientists. The first of these demarcations has three regions, each of which covers a major portion of the nation. The Ohio and Mississippi Rivers are the principal boundaries of the *North, Southeast,* and *Transmississippi.*[12] Because of economic affinities, however, the states of Arkansas and Louisiana are included in the Southeast instead of in Transmississippi. The second demarcation accepts the principal boundaries of the first, but subdivides two of the major regions in order to obtain greater precision. The North is divided into *New England, Middle Atlantic,* and *Great Lakes;* Southeast remains as it is; and Transmississippi is divided into *Plains, Mountains, Southwest,* and *Far West.* The third demarcation divides the states into the four major regions that are employed by the U.S. Bureau of the Census. *Northeast* includes New England plus the urban-industrial states of New York, New

12 Demarcations 1 and 2 are similar to those used in Harvey S. Perloff, Edgar S. Dunn, Jr., Eric E. Lamphard, and Richard F. Muth, *Regions, Resources, and Economic Growth* (Baltimore: Johns Hopkins University Press, 1960). While the nature of Perloff's demarcations remains unchanged, his "West" is called "Transmississippi" in order to eliminate its confusion with other designations used below. Likewise the region that the Bureau of the Census names "West" is called "Transplains."

Jersey, and Pennsylvania. *North Central* combines the Great Lakes and Plains regions of the second demarcation. *South* includes the 11 states of the Confederacy plus the border states of Delaware, Maryland, West Virginia, Kentucky, and Oklahoma. Finally, *Transplains* includes the states of the mountain, desert, and Pacific Coast areas.

Notice that the use of these three demarcations permits us to examine various combinations of states and various assignments of "border states" for their political saliency. In one grouping we test Delaware and Maryland with Southern states; elsewhere, we test them with the Northern and Middle Atlantic regions. The states surrounding the Great Lakes are treated as a region by themselves, as regional partners with eastern states in the North, and with other midwestern states in Northcentral. States in the Southwest are also treated at one time by themselves, and elsewhere as components of a greater west (Transmississippi). In yet other groupings, the four states of the Southwest are divided between a more westerly region (Transplains) and a southern region (South). New England is tested both as a distinct entity, as a component with three of its immediate neighbors (Northeast), and as a part of the 16-state greater North.

On the basis of preliminary research, three additional regions were chosen for treatment in this book. Two of them grow out of the Civil War and the subsequent fixation of regional scholars on its cultural and political residue. The Confederacy, the region identical to that used by V. O. Key, includes the eleven states that seceded from the Union and have subsequently formed the center of the "Southern" way of life and politics. The Border states—the region that surrounds the Confederacy—either were slave states before the War or (in the case of Oklahoma) enforced statewide racial segregation during most of the twentieth century. This Border region is somewhat larger than that considered by John Fenton.[13] By evaluating its political saliency, we can determine if Fenton's claims for the distinctiveness of his region extend to all the states that typically carry the label of Border states.

The final region added to our list is the Upper Middle

13 See note 4 above.

MAP I.   *A Regional Demarcation with Three Groupings*

MAP II.   *A Regional Demarcation with Eight Groupings*

MAP III. *A Regional Demarcation with Four Groupings*

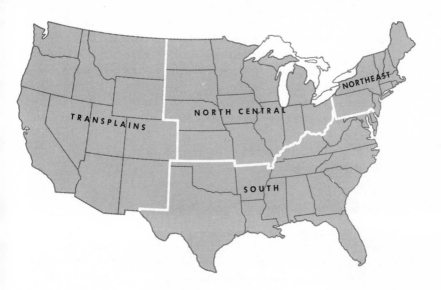

MAP IV. *Three Additional Regions*

West. Its members—Michigan, Wisconsin, Minnesota, and North Dakota—were grouped initially because of a peculiarity that is mentioned often: each has a political party that is noted for its liberal ideology. In Michigan it is the Democratic party of university intellectuals and Walter Reuther's United Auto Workers; in Wisconsin it is the Democratic party outgrowth from Robert LaFollette's Progressive party; in Minnesota it is the Farmer-Labor party, identified with Hubert Humphrey; and in North Dakota it is the Non-Partisan League.

Maps I, II, III, and IV depict each of the 17 regions that are described here.

Measures of Politics and Public Policy

The measures of politics and policy that are described here are the *dependent variables* of this study: "variables," in that their values vary from one state to another; "dependent," in that their values are expected to depend on the regional affiliation or the economic characteristics of each state. Insofar as each state's regional affiliation and economic characteristics are conceived to be potential influences upon the dependent variables, region and economic characteristics are the *independent variables* of the study—"independent," in this context, because they are not conceived to vary in response to other factors.[14]

Two principal standards are employed in the selection of dependent variables: (1) they should cover the field of characteristics that other political scientists have considered in their studies of the American states; and (2) they must be measurable in precise terms. By meeting the first standard, we can compare our own findings about the importance of region with the claims of other political scientists who—without testing for region—have claimed that the same dependent variables respond mainly to the economic characteristics of states (see Appendix A). Moreover, we can systematize the claims of

14 While it is likely that economic characteristics do vary in response to certain measurable phenomena, this dependence of economic characteristics is outside the focus of this analysis.

political scientists who have studied state politics on a regional basis, but who have limited their usefulness by failing to quantify their measures of politics or by failing to consider more than one region.

The standard of quantification will exclude certain aspects of politics that do not lend themselves to crisp measurement. The ideological orientation of political elites, the loyalty that citizens feel toward state or federal governments, the respect for the rights of minority groups—these are only three examples of potentially important regional traits that do not appear in our quantitative analyses. However, the insistence on precisely measured dependent variables will allow us to answer important questions about the relative distinctiveness of various regions, and the relative importance of regionalism with respect to our political variables. We could not employ the statistical tests that will permit answers to these questions if we tolerated imprecise assessments of state politics.[15] Thus, we shall opt for precision and expect to pay the price of omitting important traits from our findings.

Each of the variables used in this book came from widely available publications of the U.S. Government, private research staffs, or scholarly publications. The data for the "current" analysis pertains to the 1960–1962 period, selected on account of the 1960 *Census of Population* and the 1962 *Census of Governments*. The data employed in the analysis of change in regionalism (Chapter 4) pertains to a variety of years during the 1902–1962 period, depending on the availability of data. The source of each variable is given in Appendix B.

Twenty measures of state political characteristics assess various aspects of relationships between citizens and their governments: the incidence of voter turnout; the intensity of two-party competition; the equity of urban-rural apportionment in state legislatures; the activism of legislators; and the relative number and professionalism of state legislators and administrators. Presumably, high scores on these characteristics mean that state residents have a greater than average oppor-

---

[15] The dependent variables meet the demands of the statistics to be employed: they are interval in nature; they approximate normal distributions; and all two-variable relationships are linear.

tunity to influence the nature of government decisions. A high incidence of voting seems likely to increase officials' sensitivity to the needs or desires of the electorate; with intense competition between two political parties, voters are likely to be offered alternative programs and a minority party to supervise the behavior of the major party while it holds office; with equitably apportioned legislative districts the voters in the most populous areas should have a fair opportunity to gain a hearing for their wants; and with active and professionally inclined legislators and administrators the people are most likely to enjoy accurate assessments of their needs and efficient service from public officials.[16] By measuring several aspects of the citizen-government relationship, this book will examine in the regional context some of the governmental phenomena that have long been the subject of popular concern and scholarly analysis.

Two of the dependent variables measure the incidence of voter turnout for major statewide elections. These are:

1. Percentage of voting age population voting in the 1962 election for U.S. Representative (U.S. Rep turnout).
2. Percentage of voting age population voting in the 1962 (or 1960) election for Governor (Governor turnout).

Of the seven measures of inter-party competition, four measure the percentage of the vote received by the winning party at recent elections or the percentage of seats held in the state legislature by the major party; three others measure competition over a span of recent years by calculating the proportion of the time that the major party has had control of certain key positions in state government. In each case, *high state scores on these variables indicate low party competition;* it is the low scores (approaching 50 percent) that indicate high inter-party competition.

16 See Dye, *op. cit.;* Dawson and Robinson, *op. cit.;* and John G. Grumm, "Structure and Policy in the Legislature," a paper presented at the Southwestern Social Science Association Meeting, Dallas, March 1967.

3. Percentage of state legislature's lower house seats occupied by major party, 1962 [17] (lower house competition).

4. Percentage of state legislature's upper house seats occupied by major party, 1962 (upper house competition).

5. Percentage of votes received by major party in 1962 elections for U.S. Representative (U.S. Rep competition).

6. Percentage of votes received by winner in 1962 (or 1960) gubernatorial election (Governor competition).

7. Number of years in 1952–1962 period major party held Governor's office (Governor tenure).

8. Number of years in 1954–1962 period major party held control of the lower house of the legislature (lower house tenure).

9. Number of years in 1954–1962 period major party held control of the upper house of the legislature (upper house tenure).

Three indices measure the equity of apportionment in state legislative districts prior to the upheavals touched off by the 1962 *Baker* v. *Carr* decision by the United States Supreme Court. The most complex (the Schubert-Press index) assesses apportionment equity by combining inverted coefficients of variability with measures of skewness in the distribution of district populations and kurtosis (peakedness) of their distribution; thus, the Schubert-Press index considers several dimensions of the deviation from the statewide norm shown by legislative districts. The Dauer-Kelsay index adds the residents in the smallest-population districts until it finds the minimum percentage of a state's population that can elect a majority of legislators in each house. The David-Eisenberg index shows the equity of apportionment by computing the relative value of a vote cast in the most populous urban county of each state. It does so by determining the ratio of this constituency's population to that of the average constituency population for each

[17] In recording variables 3, 4, 8, and 9 for the nonpartisan Nebraska and Minnesota legislatures, it was assumed that minimum distortion would occur from the substitution of scores from comparable competition measures for the office of Governor.

house and then averaging the ratios for both houses; the greater the ratio, the more equitable the state apportionment. For each measure of legislative apportionment, a high score signifies equitable districting.

10. Schubert-Press index (S-P apportionment).
11. Dauer-Kelsay index (D-K apportionment).
12. David-Eisenberg index (D-E apportionment).

Eight dependent variables measure the relative number of state legislators and administrators plus aspects of their activism and professionalism. The indicators of active state legislators show the numbers of bills introduced and passed in a recent session and the number of days in the session. The indicators of professionalism assess salary levels and the coverage of state merit systems.

13. Number of state legislators, 1962 (legislators).
14. Number of state and local government employees per 10,000 population, 1962 (employees).
15. Number of bills introduced in a 1962 or 1963 session of legislature (bills introduced).
16. Number of bills passed in a 1962 or 1963 session of legislature (bills passed).
17. Number of days in a 1962 or 1963 session of the legislature (legislative session).
18. Average compensation of state legislators during 1962 or 1963 (legislators' compensation).
19. Average salary of state and local government employees, 1962 (employees' salary).
20. Index of merit-system coverage of state government employees, 1962 (merit-system coverage).

Forty-one variables measure the nature of *public policies* that flow from the politics of each state. They assess levels of *government expenditures* and *revenues* of various types; *public services* in the major categories of education, highways, and welfare; and *intergovernmental relations* between federal, state, and local agencies. Taken together, these measures of policy indicate the level of benefits associated with state and local government programs, the costs of these programs to state residents, and the ways in which state and local governments have chosen to finance their activities.

Eight of the dependent variables indicate the level of state, or state and local, government spending per capita—both in total and for the major services of education, highways, and public welfare. Previous research has found that high (or low) state government expenditures and high (or low) state plus local government expenditures do not occur together for the same states. The two types of spending variables reflect different political processes, so they are both tested for their responsiveness to regional phenomena.[18]

> 21. Total state government expenditures per capita, 1962 (total state expend).
> 22. State government expenditures per capita for education, 1962 (state educ expend).
> 23. State government expenditures per capita for highways, 1962 (state high expend).
> 24. State government expenditures per capita for public welfare, 1962 (state welfare expend).
> 25. Total state and local government expenditures per capita, 1962 (total s+l expend).
> 26. State and local government expenditures per capita for education, 1962 (s+l educ expend).
> 27. State and local government expenditures per capita for highways, 1962 (s+l high expend).
> 28. State and local government expenditures per capita for public welfare, 1962 (s+l welfare expend).

Nine dependent variables measure various aspects of state and local government revenue systems. Two of these assess the relative *effort* demonstrated by total tax systems by showing the percentage of personal income taken from state residents. This is not an entirely satisfactory measure of tax effort, insofar as most states do not rely on the personal income tax as

[18] See my *Spending in the American States* (Chicago: Rand McNally, 1968), chapters I, IV, and V.

their primary source of revenue. However, personal income is the most readily available indicator of citizens' economic resources, and the percentage of that income paid in taxes suggests the willingness of officials and citizens to use their resources in support of governmental activities. Six other variables show the per capita amounts of state and local revenues raised during a recent year from the major levies on real property, general sales, excises (including taxes on tobacco, alcohol, and gasoline), individual incomes, motor vehicle licenses, and current charges for services (including citizens' payments to public water supply systems, parks, colleges, and toll roads). Finally, one variable measures the per capita amount of state and local debt outstanding during 1962.

29. State tax revenues as a percentage of personal income, 1962 (state taxes).

30. State and local government tax revenues as a percentage of personal income, 1962 (s+l taxes).

31. State and local property tax revenues per capita, 1962 (property tax).

32. State and local general sales tax revenues per capita, 1962 (sales tax).

33. State and local excise tax revenues per capita, 1962 (excise tax).

34. State and local motor vehicle licenses and operators' revenues per capita, 1962 (motor vehicle tax).

35. State and local individual income tax revenue per capita, 1962 (income tax).

36. State and local revenues from current service charges per capita, 1962 (current charges).

37. State and local debt per capita, 1962 (debt).

Four indices of intergovernmental financial relations pertaining to each state measure transactions between state and local governments, as well as transactions between each of these governments and the federal government.

38. Percentage of state and local government revenues allocated to state agencies, 1962 (revenue to state).

39. Percentage of state and local government revenues coming from non-local sources, 1962 (revenue from non-local).

40. Percentage of state government revenue coming from the federal government, 1962 (federal/state revenue).

41. Percentage of state and local government revenue coming from the federal government, 1962 (federal/s+1 revenue).

Twenty dependent variables purport to measure public service levels in the fields of education, highways, and public welfare. Although the assessment of service quality or quantity is a task that has defied widespread acceptance by political scientists, it is possible to measure certain aspects of each major service. The measures that are used here claim to do no more; they are offered humbly as indicators of specific aspects of each service rather than as overall indicators of education, highway, or welfare activities in each state.[19]

Four of the twenty are measures of educational service, showing the frequency with which state populations use various programs, including school lunches, vocational education, vocational rehabilitation, and elementary and secondary schools. The higher a state scores on these measures, the more its educational programs seem to be meeting the needs of its citizens. In the case of high-school completions, for example, high scores suggest that the programs offered by schools attract their clients to remain until graduation. Another measure of educational service shows the percentage of state candidates who pass a national examination: the selective service mental test. Presumably, this measure reflects the success with which school systems throughout each state provide a minimum of intellectual skills to their students.

Three measures of highway services show the mileage of certain types of roads in relation to population. Population is seen as a reliable measure of highway traffic in most parts of

[19] For evidence that it is shortsighted to employ measures of spending as proxies for measures of public services, see my "Government Expenditures and Public Services in the American States," *American Political Science Review*, LXI (December 1967), 1066–1077.

the United States; [20] therefore, road mileage relative to population stands as a measure of transportation needs that are being met by state and local highway systems. One highway measure assesses the percentage of each state's interstate highway allocation completed by a certain date; this should gauge the capacity of state and local highway officials to work their way through the complex problems of route planning, negotiation with the U.S. Bureau of Public Roads, land-taking, and construction. Another measure shows the incidence of paved roads in each state and reflects the thoroughness with which state and local agencies have provided at least the rudiments of modern service to their rural populations. And finally, one measure of highway deaths purports to assess the safety of each state's roads, and may reflect the efficiency of a state's highway patrol as well as road maintenance and the design criteria of highway engineers.

In the welfare field, four variables assess the generosity of the major public assistance programs; four others report the coverage of relevant populations by each public assistance program.

42. Percentage of school enrollment participating in the federal school lunch program, 1962 (school lunch).

43. Total enrollment in federally aided vocational education per 10,000 population, 1962 (vocational education).

44. Number of persons in process of vocational rehabilitation per 10,000 population, 1962 (rehab process).

45. Number of persons completing vocational rehabilitation per 10,000 population, 1962 (rehab completion).

46. Percentage of eighth graders in 1958 graduating from high school in 1962 (school completion).

47. Percentage of selective service registrants passing mental examination, 1962 (exam success).

48. Mileage per capita of all roads, 1962 (total roads).

49. Mileage per rural resident of rural roads, 1962 (rural roads).

[20] Philip H. Burch, *Highway Revenue and Expenditure Policy in the United States* (New Brunswick: Rutgers University Press, 1962), p. 23.

50. Mileage per urban resident of municipal roads, 1962 (urban roads).

51. Percentage of designated interstate mileage open to traffic by 1962 (open I system).

52. Percentage of farms on improved (not dirt) roads, 1959 (paved roads).

53. State resident per motor vehicle death, 1962 (road safety).

54. Average payment per recipient of Aid to Families of Dependent Children, 1962 (AFDC payment).

55. Average payment per recipient of Old Age Assistance, 1962 (OAA payment).

56. Average payment per recipient of Aid to the Blind, 1962 (AB payment).

57. Average payment per recipient of Aid to the Permanently and Totally Disabled, 1962 (APTD payment).

58. Incidence of AFDC recipients among families with incomes of less than $2,000, 1962 (AFDC recipients).

59. Incidence of OAA recipients among people over 65 and with incomes of less than $2,000, 1962 (OAA recipients).

60. Incidence of AB recipients among people with incomes of less than $2,000, 1962 (AB recipients).

61. Incidence of APTD recipients among people with incomes of less than $2,000, 1962 (APTD recipients).

Techniques of Analysis

Once each state's scores on these 61 dependent variables are recorded, deriving answers to the principal questions in this book requires four operations: (1) computing averages for the states in each region on each of the dependent variables; (2) computing a measure of intra-regional homogeneity on each dependent variable; (3) showing the strength of the economic explanation for the dependent variables; and (4) testing for the relative influence of states' economic characteristics and non-economic regional characteristics on the dependent variables.

By themselves regional averages (arithmetic means) on

each dependent variable will test some of the allegations about politics in each region, showing, for example, the differences between various Southern regions and other sections of the country on the measures of party competition, voter turnout, and the generosity of public programs. Yet these averages will not support claims about the distinctness of any region. Averages are notoriously prone to distortion by individual cases that differ greatly from the central tendency. Because many of the regions considered here include less than a half dozen states, their average scores on any dependent variable may suffer great distortion from one deviant state. The question about regional distinctiveness can be resolved only by an operation that tests for homogeneity with respect to the regional average. A device that is both useful and easy to understand, the *coefficient of variability,* equals the regional average of a dependent variable divided into the regional standard deviation:

$$\frac{\text{s.d.X}}{\text{X}} = V$$

The standard deviation of a variable measures the magnitude of spread in scores around their mean; because the magnitude of spread is conditioned by the size of the mean, the standard deviation by itself would vary from region to region partly in accordance with the size of the regional mean. The coefficient of variability shows the magnitude of spread in proportion to the mean. *Low scores on the coefficient of variability* indicate a *tight clustering* of state scores around the regional mean, and therefore relatively great homogeneity within the region. By examining the coefficients of variability for each region and each dependent variable, it should be possible to identify those regional groupings that are most distinctive in their politics. This technique should help resolve the problem of ambiguous border states. By looking at different groupings of the Southern states, for example, it should be evident from the lowest coefficients of variability which particular combination of states is most distinctive (homogeneous) on each of the dependent variables.

Coefficients of variability will also be useful in examining changes in regionalism over time. In Chapter 4, such coefficients demonstrate that the distinctiveness of certain regional traits has indeed changed over the course of this century.

After we have used a comparison of regional means and coefficients of variability to discern those groupings of states that are highly distinctive as regions, we shall test the validity of economic explanations for state politics. Thus, we must identify several economic measures and define the procedures that will assess their relevance for the dependent variables.

The economic measures assess three different aspects of welfare—personal income, living conditions, and total resources—that previous studies have found to be relevant for voter turnout, party competition, government expenditures, and other policies of state and local governments.[21] The specific variables—to be considered along with "regional affiliation" as the independent variables of this study—are:

(a) per capita personal income, 1962
(b) percentage of population living in urban areas, 1960
(c) total personal income, 1962

Variable *a* is considered to measure individual welfare, variable *b* indicates a pattern of settlement reflecting resources and life-styles, and variable *c* shows the magnitude of economic resources within each state. Each of these characteristics shows strong relationships with other measures of individual welfare, resources, and "sophisticated" life-styles; each seems to affect the inclination of state populations to voter turnout, party competition, legislative activism, professionalism in the legislature and bureaucracy, and high scores on many measures of state and local government expenditures, revenues, and public service levels. Generally speaking, the states that score high on any one of the economic measures also score high on the others. However, as the coefficients of simple correlation (in Table 2–2) indicate, there is considerable "slippage" among economic characteristics. For this reason, we shall employ all three economic variables in the analysis of economic *vs.* regional influences on state politics.

The analyses of Chapter 5 employ *coefficients of simple*

21 See Appendix A, pp. 179–183.

TABLE 2–2. COEFFICIENTS OF SIMPLE CORRELATION AMONG THREE MEASURES OF STATE ECONOMIC CHARACTERISTICS

	A	B	C
a) Per Capita Personal Income	1.00	.44*	.69**
b) Urbanization		1.00	.58**
c) Total Personal Income			1.00

* significant at the .01 level
** significant at the .001 level

correlation, partial correlation, and *multiple determination* for the purpose of assessing how the economic variables are related to each measure of politics and public policy. Coefficients of simple correlation (product moment) show the strength and direction of relationships between each economic variable (e.g., per capita personal income) and each dependent variable (e.g., voter turnout). If the direction of the relationship is positive, it means that high (or low) scores on one variable are associated with high (or low) scores on the other variable. Thus, states scoring high (or low) on per capita personal income would also score high (or low) on voter turnout. Where correlation coefficients are negative, they signal inverse relationships: a high score on one variable coexisting with a low score on the other variable. The magnitude of correlation coefficients ranges between 0.0 and ± 1.0. The closer the coefficient to ± 1.0, the greater the relationship between scores on the variables. In graphic terms, a simple correlation coefficient of 1.0 reflects the condition where each state's scores on the variables plotted against two axes at 90 degrees from one another form a straight line sloping upward from the horizontal. Inversely, a coefficient of −1.0 reflects a straight line sloping down from left to right. A correlation coefficient approaching 0.0 reflects a plot that shows no linear relationship between two variables.

Coefficients of simple correlation do not indicate whether relationships between variables are truly *independent;* that is, they cannot determine whether a relationship between per capita personal income and turnout indicates an elemental relationship between personal well-being and political participation, or merely reflects a more basic relationship involving a third variable, such as urbanization. If the incidence of urban settlement in a state has powerful relationships with both per capita personal income and voter turnout, then the relationship between per capita income and turnout might reflect nothing more than the existence of the common factor. Coefficients of partial correlation help to indicate the independence of relationships. When used in a multi-variable problem they show the strength of relationships between two variables while taking into account their common relationships with others. As used in Chapter 5, coefficients of partial correlation indicate which of the three measures of economic development shows the most basic relationship with each of the dependent variables.

Neither coefficients of simple correlation nor those of partial correlation indicate the success of several independent variables combined in explaining interstate differences in a dependent variable. Coefficients of multiple determination (R^2) do show the total explanatory power of several independent variables. We shall use these coefficients in Chapter 5, to show the proportion of variation explained by the three economic indicators taken together, but also to indicate the proportion of variation that is *not* accounted for by the economic measures. For our purposes, these coefficients demonstrate the need to look beyond our economic characteristics as explanations for state politics and public policy.

Chapter 5 also includes a statistical comparison of two sorts of explanations for state politics: economic explanations versus an explanation that relies upon non-economic traits of the regions. Two separate *analysis of covariance* techniques provide the basis for judging the relative influence of economic and non-economic regional influences. One analysis of covariance determines if a region shows a significant association with each dependent variable that is independent of its relationship with the three economic measures. In effect, this test determines if the inter-regional differences in a measure are accounted for statistically by inter-regional differences in economic characteristics. To the extent that economics does *not* account for inter-regional differences in politics or public policies, then non-economic aspects of the region will appear salient.[22]

The second analysis of covariance measures the magnitude of the economic-political relationships while controlling for region. This test determines the strength of relationships between economic characteristics and dependent variables, within regions and nationwide; to the extent that economic-political relationships are as strong within regions as they are nationwide, then the analysis shows the saliency of the economic variables.

It is possible that both region and economic characteristics show significant relationships with a dependent variable while controlling for one another. Conceptually, this may happen when scores on a measure of politics show some interstate variation that depends on economic characteristics independent of region, and some variation that depends on regional factors that are other than economic. We might find, for example, that Southern states show low party competition no matter what their level of economic development, while party competition among the New England states varies with their level of economic development.

Where the findings of a covariance analysis show that non-economic characteristics of regions have important relationships with a dependent variable, our task will not be over. Regionalism itself is not a satisfactory explanation for state politics or policies. The question to be faced is: *What non-economic characteristics of regions are responsible for their distinctive scores on the dependent variables?*

Ultimately the answer to this question will require a search of regional culture and history, and a study of interstate communications among political elites. In this book we shall make some speculative assessments about the phenomena likely to produce each region's distinctive score. We shall be guided, however, by the identification of those regions where economic

22 The procedure followed in computing this statistic can be found in Hubert M. Blalock, *Social Statistics* (New York: McGraw Hill, 1959), pp. 361–362, 373, 380; the computer program employed is "Analysis of Covariance with Multiple Covariates: BMD04V," in *Biomedical Computer Programs* (Los Angeles: University of California Health Sciences Computing Facility, 1965).

characteristics are *least successful* in accounting for the political or policy traits. To do this, we shall first estimate each region's score on a dependent variable by the regression formula:

$$Y = a + b_1X_1 + b_2X_2 + b_3X_3$$

In this formula, Y equals the estimated regional average on the dependent variable; X_1, X_2, and X_3 are the regional average for each economic variable; the a and the b's are constants determined by a 48-state regression of the dependent variable with the three economic variables.[23] The use of this formula with regional scores on the independent variables will produce an estimate (Y) of the dependent variable for the region. By comparing this regional estimate with the actual regional average for the dependent variable according to the simple formula

$$\frac{\text{actual regional mean of Y}}{\text{regional mean estimated for Y}}$$

we can identify the regions in which the dependent variable does not stand in its usual relationship with the economic variables. The more this ratio departs from 1.00 (obtained where the actual regional score equals the estimated score), the region's score on a measure of politics will be greater (or less) than is generally associated with its level of per capita personal income, urbanization, and total personal income.

When we come to the explanations for regional peculiarities on measures of state politics and policy we shall leave behind the security of precisely measured variables, analyses of covariance, and regression formulae. Our only firm data will indicate that political and policy traits of certain regions are associated with non-economic characteristics of those regions —characteristics we shall find by looking to each region's culture and history for experiences that seem to account for its current traits. While our inquiries may produce some insights into the origin of regional traits, the focus of this book will

[23] In this 48-state regression, when the b's are multiplied with nationwide averages for their respective independent variables, these products are added together and then added to a constant a (also determined by the 48-state regression). The sum will approximate the 48-state average for the dependent variable.

preclude a thorough exploration of regional histories and culture. Most of the work will be directed at identifying regional traits, selecting the regional groupings that are most distinctive politically, and testing the regional findings for the influence of economic characteristics. The historical-cultural explanation of residual regional differences will be limited in scope; it will use a few illustrative cases to examine the analytical value of looking toward culture and history in regional analyses.

Summary

In combining the 48 contiguous states into 17 regions, we shall make an effort to take account of the diverse characteristics that might cement nearby states into regional partnerships: for example, immigration from common sources, similar terrain, the joint experience of Civil War and Reconstruction, shared markets, common natural resources, and the sharing of ideology across state borders. Partly because of these different bases for regional affiliation, individual states show in themselves the traits of several regions. They represent the border state problems that preclude a single division of 48 states into one fixed set of regions. In an attempt to deal with the border state problems, we employ multiple demarcations that provide alternative placements for several of the states.

Although the use of 17 regions and 61 dependent variables threatens to become unwieldy of its own accord, we shall find that the topic at hand is indeed unwieldy. The saliency of regional borders varies with that aspect of politics or public policy that is subject to investigation. On some dimensions of politics, for example, it is necessary to distinguish between the Mountain and Far Western areas; but on other dimensions it is better to speak of the more inclusive regions of Transplains or Transmississippi. The use of 17 regions should illuminate much of the richness in regional patterns throughout the United States. Although some scholars might feel that this book could profit from additional groupings of the states, the economics of research and clear presentation argue against any further divisions.

3

REGIONAL PATTERNS
IN STATE POLITICS
AND PUBLIC POLICIES

This chapter begins the identification of regional patterns in politics and public policies, taking the 17 regions and 61 dependent variables described in Chapter 2 and attempting to discern the distinctive characteristics of each region.

By focusing on the identification of *distinctive* regional characteristics, we are claiming something more than a simple descriptive accomplishment; we not only seek to define the relative position of each region on each measure of politics or policy, but also seek to determine which of the regions outlined in Chapter 2 are most worthy of analysis. There are two principal attributes of a distinctive region: its states must differ politically from nearby states that are not part of the region, and its states must show considerable uniformity with respect to the regional traits. If the traits of a "region" are not clearly different from those of nearby states they hardly warrant special consideration, and if states within a "region" differ so much from one another that they vary widely from the regional average, their diffuseness would appear to disqualify them from regional status.

We shall use two simple tests in judging the distinctiveness of the regions described in Chapter 2. First, their mean scores (the arithmetic averages of their member states' scores) on each dependent variable are compared to nationwide means and the means of other regional groupings. Second, regional coefficients of variability are compared for the purpose of identifying those regions that show the most uniformity on each dependent variable. The means and coefficients of variability of the Border States, for example, are compared to those of the Old Confederacy and the Northcentral and Northeastern regions to see if John Fenton was correct in viewing the Border States as intermediate between the South and non-South. In a similar fashion, the scores of the Upper Middle West are compared to those of the Northcentral region in order to test the wisdom of carving the Upper Middle West out of the inclusive Northcentral region. And New England's scores are compared to those of the more inclusive Northeast to determine if the six states east of New York warrant separate treatment.

It is fair to warn the reader at the outset that any search for "clean" or "simple" regional patterns will be frustrated. There are clear differences between regions on most measures of politics, but those differences are not of a type to carry over in any consistent pattern from one dependent variable to another. Thus, some regions are highly distinct from their neighbors on some aspects of politics but not on others. The Border States, for example, differ from the Confederacy on measures of voter turnout but not on measures of legislative apportionment, tax effort, and certain types of educational service. On the educational services that are supported by federal aid (school lunches, vocational education, and vocational rehabilitation) the regional border that follows the Ohio River is more salient than that which separates the Confederacy from the Border States. This complexity repeats itself on a number of traits and for a number of regional boundaries. The political map of the United States does not reveal sharp regional boundaries that are consistent from one trait to another.

The multi-dimensionality of political regionalism is helpful at the same time that it is confusing. Because there are no clear regional borders that prevail across all (or most) topics of inquiry, it is apparent that no simple set of historical experiences left their mark on the wide range of dependent variables that are considered here. Because of this it is necessary to identify a myriad of stimulants that have operated in different regional contexts upon different aspects of politics. But the specificity of the regional differences aids in the search for these stimulants. By knowing that the Border States are like the South in certain educational policies but not in their levels of voter turnout, for example, it is possible to gain insight into the regional processes by looking at the factors relevant to each trait as well as to each region. In this way the variegated map of political regionalism provides more clues to its own explanation than would a simpler map showing clear regional boundaries from one trait to another.

This chapter confines itself to the *identification* of distinctive regional traits, and will not dwell on the *explanation* for them. Because it is likely that many regional peculiarities reflect nothing more complicated than current economic conditions, our efforts at explanation wait until we test for the basis of our regional findings.

The simple statistical techniques of this chapter are commensurate with its unambitious goals. The comparison of means and coefficients of variability provides information about the regions that score high and low on each dependent variable, and are more or less uniform in their characteristics. The findings provide some measure of intellectual progress over the descriptions of individual regions. However, it will be left to later chapters to make the major advances by testing the economic explanation of regional findings, and identifying those regional traits that do not merely reflect current economic conditions.

The Distinctiveness of Regionalism

A comparison of regional with national coefficients of variability provides some welcome evidence that we are not wasting our time with this investigation of political regions. The data (given in Table 3-1) show that regions tend to be more

TABLE 3–1.   MEANS AND COEFFICIENTS OF VARIABILITY,*

	U.S.	NORTH	NOEAST	NEW ENG	MID ATL	GRT LAKES	PLAINS
1) U.S. Rep Turn **	46.98	55.41	56.40	57.67	51.42	56.70	54.24
	(.330)	(.122)	(.102)	(.097)	(.164)	(.098)	(.137)
2) Gov Turn	52.70	59.76	58.29	59.26	56.64	63.47	59.43
	(.321)	(.159)	(.103)	(.105)	(.198)	(.188)	(.136)
3) Lower House Comp	70.29	62.80	64.12	68.92	62.91	55.36	63.67
	(.229)	(.167)	(.156)	(.123)	(.200)	(.091)	(.172)
4) Upper House Comp	72.76	65.24	66.87	69.92	63.40	61.45	66.00
	(.233)	(.143)	(.164)	(.149)	(.151)	(.097)	(.212)
5) U.S. Rep Comp	59.70	53.95	55.06	57.42	52.02	51.72	56.54
	(.176)	(.075)	(.087)	(.070)	(.050)	(.047)	(.071)
6) Gov Comp	57.47	52.86	52.41	52.13	53.26	53.32	53.20
	(.204)	(.059)	(.059)	(.068)	(.043)	(.071)	(.056)
7) Gov Tenure	9.33	8.50	8.89	8.67	8.80	8.00	8.29
	(.240)	(.219)	(.254)	(.279)	(.203)	(.176)	(.258)
8) Lower House Tenure	9.13	9.13	9.33	9.67	9.20	8.40	8.86
	(.152)	(.119)	(.120)	(.085)	(.412)	(.106)	(.230)
9) Upper House Tenure	9.04	9.13	8.89	8.33	10.00	9.20	8.57
	(.173)	(.159)	(.198)	(.236)	(.000)	(.120)	(.232)
10) Schubert-Press	47.70	59.35	62.07	59.70	56.30	61.98	36.77
	(.507)	(.323)	(.317)	(.405)	(.294)	(.303)	(.789)
11) Dauer-Kelsay	67.10	66.74	68.90	67.35	60.24	72.52	70.84
	(.208)	(.250)	(.233)	(.284)	(.290)	(.186)	(.134)
12) David-Eisenberg	63.56	83.25	86.11	88.00	78.20	82.60	54.57
	(.363)	(.128)	(.107)	(.120)	(.133)	(.127)	(.285)
13) Legislators	164.19	202.81	243.33	273.50	154.40	166.40	148.43
	(.471)	(.468)	(.419)	(.366)	(.563)	(.244)	(.373)
14) Bills Intro	2257.69	3556.56	4737.78	3306.00	5452.40	1961.40	1371.29
	(1.233)	(1.234)	(1.200)	(.978)	(1.306)	(.424)	(.822)
15) Bills Pass	754.31	869.13	960.56	901.50	1002.00	697.40	510.29
	(.706)	(.636)	(.656)	(.652)	(.618)	(.746)	(.376)
16) Legis Session	118.17	140.56	122.00	130.50	111.60	181.60	117.29
	(.475)	(.491)	(.498)	(.471)	(.442)	(.473)	(.434)

* Indicated by the figures in parentheses.
** The complete title of each dependent variable is shown in Chapter 2, pp. 34–41.

BY REGION ON 61 DEPENDENT VARIABLES

NO-CENTRAL	UPP MID-WEST	BORDER	SO-EAST	SOUTH	CONFED	SO-WEST	MOUNTNS	FAR WEST	TRANS-PLAINS	TRANS-MISS
55.27	58.08***	46.18	25.84	29.74	22.20	40.05	61.32	52.90	55.30	52.91
(.119)	(.074)	(.216)	(.479)	(.465)	(.276)	(.229)	(.074)	(.072)	(.135)	(.181)
61.11	60.24	60.18	35.16	38.33	29.37	42.44	65.84	59.13	59.84	57.57
(.164)	(.083)	(.267)	(.540)	(.500)	(.414)	(.238)	(.106)	(.136)	(.167)	(.197)
60.27	54.33	71.85	89.95	87.80	94.16	79.46	59.38	57.13	60.79	64.48
(.167)	(.093)	(.125)	(.138)	(.136)	(.085)	(.188)	(.102)	(.140)	(.148)	(.191)
64.11	65.65	66.21	90.66	88.06	96.73	89.89	56.63	63.94	64.74	68.03
(.172)	(.167)	(.212)	(.165)	(.182)	(.062)	(.078)	(.088)	(.125)	(.185)	(.219)
54.53	51.53	56.93	71.08	68.16	73.22	60.58	54.36	59.88	56.83	57.47
(.076)	(.038)	(.049)	(.195)	(.195)	(.178)	(.110)	(.073)	(.148)	(.115)	(.101)
53.25	50.48	54.23	68.81	65.15	70.46	54.28	54.66	56.05	55.03	54.35
(.059)	(.014)	(.050)	(.278)	(.271)	(.272)	(.019)	(.027)	(.130)	(.076)	(.066)
8.17	8.00	9.33	11.67	11.00	12.00	8.50	9.20	8.50	8.56	8.60
(.220)	(.204)	(.222)	(.099)	(.163)	(.000)	(.296)	(.291)	(.118)	(.236)	(.240)
8.67	8.75	10.00	10.00	10.00	10.00	10.00	7.20	8.50	8.18	8.60
(.186)	(.171)	(.000)	(.000)	(.000)	(.000)	(.000)	(.153)	(.226)	(.203)	(.205)
8.83	9.25	10.00	10.00	10.00	10.00	10.00	7.60	7.50	8.00	8.40
(.186)	(.162)	(.000)	(.000)	(.000)	(.000)	(.000)	(.220)	(.256)	(.224)	(.216)
47.28	35.93	36.72	40.68	38.82	40.64	28.80	56.46	49.28	49.34	42.60
(.582)	(.673)	(.595)	(.629)	(.601)	(.592)	(.472)	(.207)	(.660)	(.441)	(.577)
71.54	75.73	64.43	68.78	65.63	66.78	62.95	65.02	63.68	62.91	66.38
(.151)	(.104)	(.290)	(.227)	(.248)	(.224)	(.154)	(.077)	(.309)	(.187)	(.166)
66.25	70.25	61.50	52.00	52.50	49.09	38.75	58.80	66.00	58.27	54.75
(.294)	(.236)	(.306)	(.511)	(.479)	(.553)	(.318)	(.165)	(.419)	(.332)	(.330)
155.92	160.75	175.83	158.67	167.06	165.00	188.00	105.80	103.00	104.27	136.60
(.312)	(.189)	(.596)	(.224)	(.401)	(.217)	(.658)	(.250)	(.392)	(.267)	(.512)
1617.17	2281.75	1496.67	1976.25	1952.25	2128.18	1361.75	722.40	2272.75	1371.55	1387.45
(.629)	(.591)	(.428)	(.446)	(.418)	(.393)	(.339)	(.260)	(.802)	(.908)	(.805)
588.25	593.50	504.17	949.25	886.69	1040.82	435.25	339.80	974.50	574.18	545.50
(.608)	(.342)	(.660)	(.560)	(.549)	(.453)	(.341)	(.306)	(.903)	(1.015)	(.804)
144.08	174.00	123.33	100.33	109.19	109.27	138.25	70.40	123.25	99.82	110.95
(.500)	(.631)	(.304)	(.285)	(.335)	(.401)	(.435)	(.586)	(.459)	(.531)	(.485)

*** Figures underlined show the two highest-scoring and the two lowest-scoring regions on each dependent variable.

Table 3–1 (Continued)

	U.S.	NORTH	NOEAST	NEW ENG	MID ATL	GRT LAKES	PLAINS
17) Legis Compen	7105.73	11450.88	9960.44	4440.67	16060.00	15254.00	6061.71
	(.905)	(.756)	(1.001)	(1.401)	(.480)	(.486)	(.648)
18) Employees Salary	422.90	452.88	446.00	429.50	461.80	472.00	407.00
	(.140)	(.097)	(.112)	(.106)	(.093)	(.081)	(.085)
19) Employees	339.73	326.38	323.78	325.17	331.60	322.60	354.71
	(.117)	(.080)	(.098)	(.061)	(.129)	(.042)	(.077)
20) Merit System	48.43	40.74	61.90	90.61	14.43	7.19	11.81
	(.215)	(1.386)	(1.113)	(.747)	(.958)	(.571)	(.083)
21) Total St Expend	181.40	169.40	168.14	180.07	171.73	154.27	167.29
	(.229)	(.228)	(.231)	(.212)	(.293)	(.181)	(.179)
22) St Educ Expend	60.36	49.50	41.88	39.52	60.01	50.95	49.34
	(.363)	(.408)	(.305)	(.327)	(.459)	(.323)	(.316)
23) St High Expend	52.56	48.58	49.74	58.74	39.47	45.50	56.03
	(.394)	(.425)	(.557)	(.518)	(.398)	(.133)	(.276)
24) St PW Expend	23.34	20.44	22.11	24.52	17.04	18.96	21.57
	(.424)	(.325)	(.281)	(.216)	(.317)	(.407)	(.259)
25) Total SL Expend	320.10	326.10	328.90	328.00	329.40	320.60	325.90
	(.192)	(.110)	(.121)	(.119)	(.140)	(.094)	(.121)
26) SL Educ Expend	121.50	119.90	112.50	110.60	122.70	128.10	126.50
	(.215)	(.125)	(.091)	(.126)	(.106)	(.077)	(.154)
27) SL High Expend	65.10	61.40	64.80	73.80	49.90	58.00	78.40
	(.350)	(.361)	(.429)	(.432)	(.120)	(.167)	(.250)
28) SL PW Expend	26.50	24.80	26.90	28.70	21.00	24.10	26.60
	(.358)	(.280)	(.333)	(.207)	(.286)	(.250)	(.222)
29) SL Taxes	9.49	9.22	9.54	9.77	8.64	9.14	9.67
	(.117)	(.125)	(.127)	(.127)	(.117)	(.107)	(.133)
30) St Taxes	5.14	4.41	4.30	4.51	4.48	4.21	4.18
	(.241)	(.227)	(.250)	(.244)	(.289)	(.190)	(.167)
31) Prop Tax	96.80	115.90	123.80	125.30	100.90	119.70	121.10
	(.393)	(.259)	(.250)	(.200)	(.436)	(.083)	(.167)
32) Sales Tax	28.52	23.54	18.45	16.31	19.27	36.48	20.46
	(.723)	(.826)	(.957)	(1.107)	(.924)	(.600)	(.714)
33) Excise Tax	40.16	42.75	46.24	47.25	44.79	35.30	34.72
	(.248)	(.177)	(.148)	(.152)	(.113)	(.121)	(.117)

NO-CENTRAL	UPP MID-WEST	BORDER	SO-EAST	SOUTH	CONFED	SO-WEST	MOUNTNS	FAR WEST	TRANS-PLAINS	TRANS-MISS
9891.83	12883.00	6558.33	4060.42	5060.31	4833.18	5393.50	2636.00	7987.50	4705.82	5456.80
(.721)	(.722)	(.539)	(.520)	(.569)	(.620)	(.770)	(.813)	(.622)	(.876)	(.734)
434.08	470.00	398.50	361.50	373.44	361.55	416.25	426.20	517.50	463.73	435.75
(.111)	(.104)	(.080)	(.090)	(.103)	(.097)	(.118)	(.051)	(.115)	(.125)	(.130)
341.33	344.00	321.83	310.08	316.56	312.55	337.75	391.40	393.25	384.73	368.20
(.081)	(.047)	(.086)	(.083)	(.083)	(.081)	(.052)	(.124)	(.070)	(.099)	(.103)
9.88	12.17	19.06	14.60	15.95	13.27	46.38	127.00	148.00	127.00	74.89
(.800)	(.333)	(.474)	(.829)	(.750)	(1.000)	(1.522)	(1.346)	(1.628)	(1.378)	(1.870)
161.86	190.46	193.34	167.10	173.24	159.32	196.23	312.86	241.54	225.41	199.57
(.177)	(.101)	(.184)	(.200)	(.213)	(.204)	(.217)	(.186)	(.114)	(.146)	(.214)
50.01	64.67	64.13	59.22	62.07	59.22	80.23	75.05	88.32	84.30	69.74
(.304)	(.177)	(.336)	(.180)	(.240)	(.189)	(.386)	(.280)	(.157)	(.257)	(.354)
51.64	52.03	50.74	44.37	45.08	41.44	48.67	77.07	60.26	66.76	60.66
(.255)	(.160)	(.163)	(.199)	(.186)	(.154)	(.178)	(.499)	(.288)	(.421)	(.389)
20.48	19.55	30.27	23.85	24.78	22.54	31.16	23.36	28.60	25.35	25.34
(.311)	(.158)	(.515)	(.495)	(.552)	(.531)	(.573)	(.497)	(.293)	(.363)	(.424)
323.70	360.10	295.00	255.60	268.00	253.50	311.40	372.00	423.50	384.90	354.10
(.094)	(.028)	(.100)	(.141)	(.148)	(.160)	(.129)	(.189)	(.095)	(.154)	(.172)
127.20	139.90	111.10	92.80	99.70	93.40	131.00	149.40	161.10	154.40	140.10
(.154)	(.071)	(.182)	(.088)	(.200)	(.111)	(.231)	(.200)	(.063)	(.133)	(.171)
69.90	74.60	56.40	52.40	53.10	51.10	58.30	88.70	71.70	77.40	75.60
(.286)	(.125)	(.167)	(.173)	(.200)	(.200)	(.167)	(.400)	(.286)	(.375)	(.329)
25.50	27.10	31.20	25.10	25.90	23.80	31.70	27.60	30.60	28.10	28.70
(.333)	(.162)	(.667)	(.440)	(.333)	(.500)	(.667)	(.333)	(.333)	(.333)	(.345)
9.45	10.25	8.58	9.13	9.01	9.14	9.90	10.50	9.65	10.17	9.92
(.123)	(.077)	(.097)	(.122)	(.117)	(.126)	(.066)	(.053)	(.096)	(.074)	(.097)
4.19	4.93	5.61	6.14	6.00	6.01	6.19	5.28	5.48	5.60	5.12
(.250)	(.079)	(.167)	(.180)	(.167)	(.167)	(.167)	(.083)	(.167)	(.167)	(.216)
120.50	125.30	62.10	54.20	58.30	58.30	73.50	114.70	106.80	104.90	107.20
(.167)	(.077)	(.333)	(.556)	(.500)	(.500)	(.429)	(.167)	(.273)	(.273)	(.262)
27.13	21.04	28.06	33.71	29.50	30.31	32.76	23.21	49.37	36.84	29.39
(.698)	(1.250)	(.619)	(.407)	(.510)	(.451)	(.550)	(.923)	(.797)	(.791)	(.823)
34.96	34.93	40.87	40.06	41.40	40.88	34.13	36.29	50.54	39.06	38.16
(.113)	(.118)	(.148)	(.141)	(.131)	(.142)	(.431)	(.161)	(.457)	(.441)	(.343)

TABLE 3–1 (Continued)

	U.S.	NORTH	NOEAST	NEW ENG	MID ATL	GRT LAKES	PLAINS
34) MV Tax	10.09	9.54	9.31	9.57	8.86	10.19	12.80
	(.451)	(.370)	(.493)	(.590)	(.156)	(.191)	(.229)
35) Income Tax	14.73	18.06	15.65	11.67	<u>35.15</u>	8.65	13.51
	(1.123)	(1.296)	(1.326)	(1.462)	(.858)	(1.801)	(.921)
36) Cur Charges	34.52	30.88	<u>28.30</u>	<u>25.34</u>	35.45	32.96	37.40
	(.253)	(.231)	(.247)	(.201)	(.184)	(.184)	(.265)
37) Debt	375.40	458.60	470.30	424.50	<u>605.10</u>	353.00	<u>288.70</u>
	(.410)	(.392)	(.426)	(.457)	(.271)	(.200)	(.448)
38) Rev To St	41.57	37.48	40.38	45.65	34.88	<u>30.26</u>	39.51
	(.222)	(.308)	(.311)	(.233)	(.368)	(.152)	(.205)
39) Rev From Non-Loc	40.75	46.38	47.91	44.75	45.18	<u>49.54</u>	47.76
	(.239)	(.212)	(.196)	(.181)	(.348)	(.081)	(.109)
40) Fed/St	25.96	21.75	23.46	26.42	<u>16.30</u>	21.60	28.97
	(.254)	(.319)	(.358)	(.334)	(.181)	(.104)	(.199)
41) Fed/SL	16.47	12.68	13.80	16.24	<u>9.71</u>	<u>11.40</u>	15.83
	(.321)	(.402)	(.500)	(.432)	(.196)	(.061)	(.250)
42) Sch Lunch	36.45	27.49	26.71	28.50	<u>25.74</u>	28.02	41.06
	(.307)	(.221)	(.253)	(.222)	(.250)	(.229)	(.171)
43) Voc Ed	21.80	12.96	<u>10.74</u>	12.02	<u>10.91</u>	16.13	21.35
	(.460)	(.406)	(.289)	(.197)	(.606)	(.360)	(.196)
44) Rehab Proc	134.00	116.00	128.00	136.00	122.00	<u>86.83</u>	134.00
	(.607)	(.523)	(.578)	(.625)	(.353)	(.414)	(.248)
45) Rehab Complet	65.98	54.90	56.23	54.95	69.99	39.75	48.26
	(.601)	(.556)	(.571)	(.631)	(.517)	(.268)	(.104)
46) Sch Compl	69.68	73.38	70.31	66.98	74.08	<u>80.34</u>	79.66
	(.154)	(.115)	(.105)	(.100)	(.062)	(.102)	(.064)
47) Exam Success	79.67	82.91	83.02	84.13	78.54	85.82	<u>91.34</u>
	(.174)	(.056)	(.044)	(.040)	(.052)	(.041)	(.042)
48) Total Roads	6.21	3.34	3.65	4.58	<u>3.19</u>	<u>1.98</u>	6.60
	(.778)	(1.005)	(1.063)	(.959)	(1.122)	(.364)	(.418)
49) Rural Roads	85.35	35.30	<u>31.54</u>	32.15	<u>26.86</u>	47.53	138.06
	(1.045)	(.420)	(.450)	(.551)	(.209)	(.221)	(.492)
50) Urban Roads	4.96	3.35	<u>3.23</u>	3.91	<u>2.20</u>	3.81	<u>8.12</u>
	(.446)	(.411)	(.464)	(.339)	(.466)	(.315)	(.315)
51) Open I System	34.28	40.92	41.42	39.08	38.47	<u>45.57</u>	35.03
	(.435)	(.355)	(.341)	(.373)	(.506)	(.217)	(.400)

NO-CENTRAL	UPP MID-WEST	BORDER	SO-EAST	SOUTH	CONFED	SO-WEST	MOUNTNS	FAR WEST	TRANS-PLAINS	TRANS-MISS
11.71	12.04	9.46	6.23	7.49	6.72	11.42	13.50	13.58	12.75	12.85
(.239)	(.251)	(.389)	(.408)	(.459)	(.448)	(.302)	(.467)	(.465)	(.442)	(.347)
11.49	20.41	28.24	10.20	14.95	8.31	8.63	19.82	16.91	17.21	14.79
(1.164)	(.889)	(.835)	(.709)	(1.201)	(.894)	(.684)	(.632)	(1.396)	(.902)	(.936)
35.55	39.27	32.72	30.76	32.40	31.64	37.52	38.93	46.85	41.59	39.70
(.239)	(.335)	(.235)	(.154)	(.173)	(.146)	(.098)	(.235)	(.255)	(.233)	(.235)
315.50	325.70	434.60	309.00	363.90	316.30	356.30	291.50	517.60	379.80	348.70
(.344)	(.182)	(.432)	(.256)	(.389)	(.281)	(.167)	(.241)	(.365)	(.421)	(.407)
35.66	34.80	47.60	46.38	45.90	44.58	46.30	44.04	39.33	42.71	41.97
(.228)	(.329)	(.202)	(.134)	(.162)	(.132)	(.151)	(.129)	(.197)	(.154)	(.175)
48.50	45.05	33.22	32.39	32.39	33.75	33.30	39.32	40.23	38.00	41.25
(.096)	(.089)	(.263)	(.201)	(.220)	(.221)	(.274)	(.111)	(.157)	(.178)	(.191)
25.90	21.75	24.08	26.81	25.12	26.28	25.65	34.12	25.08	29.29	28.82
(.226)	(.126)	(.320)	(.147)	(.219)	(.161)	(.092)	(.208)	(.107)	(.231)	(.210)
13.99	12.58	16.79	18.96	17.79	18.35	18.54	21.95	16.39	19.47	18.02
(.286)	(.154)	(.294)	(.195)	(.222)	(.222)	(.211)	(.273)	(.188)	(.250)	(.261)
35.63	37.25	38.43	49.73	45.14	48.46	34.33	37.18	25.68	32.69	35.67
(.262)	(.358)	(.233)	(.136)	(.226)	(.183)	(.106)	(.153)	(.404)	(.268)	(.241)
19.17	23.82	19.04	31.53	29.66	34.16	24.07	22.89	25.29	22.34	23.07
(.281)	(.195)	(.387)	(.310)	(.355)	(.244)	(.461)	(.272)	(.289)	(.312)	(.287)
102.00	129.00	202.00	193.00	184.00	164.00	114.00	136.00	77.59	99.71	112.00
(.324)	(.256)	(.842)	(.577)	(.571)	(.293)	(.947)	(.426)	(.205)	(.520)	(.507)
44.71	48.72	97.45	111.00	102.00	99.97	47.71	58.91	33.43	44.85	7.84
(.200)	(.122)	(.622)	(.402)	(.441)	(.370)	(.563)	(.288)	(.364)	(.400)	(.347)
79.94	83.93	64.75	55.82	58.61	56.57	65.45	73.80	78.05	74.05	75.03
(.078)	(.090)	(.133)	(.057)	(.104)	(.060)	(.075)	(.026)	(.131)	(.099)	(.102)
89.04	89.50	75.83	58.98	63.70	58.84	80.88	93.90	89.38	89.94	89.50
(.051)	(.053)	(.104)	(.143)	(.178)	(.158)	(.055)	(.018)	(.072)	(.068)	(.068)
4.68	4.47	7.85	7.88	7.25	6.92	6.59	10.01	6.84	8.45	7.50
(.677)	(.859)	(.692)	(.647)	(.651)	(.618)	(.571)	(.587)	(1.121)	(.724)	(.645)
100.34	108.05	47.00	38.66	42.98	43.15	112.01	203.23	159.33	174.65	153.40
(.686)	(.866)	(.697)	(.303)	(.518)	(.378)	(.394)	(.616)	(1.105)	(.741)	(.686)
6.32	6.87	4.18	5.10	4.93	5.33	5.44	5.80	3.95	4.94	6.17
(.475)	(.622)	(.428)	(.305)	(.347)	(.283)	(.199)	(.245)	(.301)	(.287)	(.380)
39.42	41.79	33.00	23.60	26.57	24.59	41.71	26.07	41.23	34.03	35.37
(.338)	(.429)	(.455)	(.508)	(.519)	(.520)	(.190)	(.423)	(.439)	(.441)	(.390)

TABLE 3–1 (Continued)

	U.S.	NORTH	NOEAST	NEW ENG	MID ATL	GRT LAKES	PLAINS
52) Paved Roads	78.14	88.98	87.77	88.92	83.80	94.24	83.57
	(.190)	(.070)	(.068)	(.065)	(.065)	(.027)	(.085)
53) Road Safety	4320.00	5870.00	6650.00	6480.00	6210.00	4800.00	3760.00
	(.356)	(.276)	(.260)	(.333)	(.177)	(.171)	(.165)
54) AFDC	125.66	146.67	151.74	147.03	144.18	148.73	138.60
	(.301)	(.218)	(.196)	(.203)	(.248)	(.253)	(.187)
55) OAA	76.89	81.98	83.38	81.71	78.97	85.32	86.99
	(.214)	(.147)	(.151)	(.176)	(.164)	(.113)	(.152)
56) AB	83.31	91.03	96.32	100.25	82.18	88.79	89.20
	(.256)	(.207)	(.237)	(.261)	(.170)	(.083)	(.201)
57) APTD	76.04	91.49	92.23	92.63	83.28	98.33	81.03
	(.319)	(.228)	(.264)	(.279)	(.262)	(.134)	(.225)
58) AFDC Recip ****	1.57	1.93	2.06	1.74	2.52	1.57	.9366
	(.548)	(.482)	(.563)	(.750)	(.155)	(.359)	(.277)
59) OAA Recip	2.72	1.35	1.72	2.50	.86	.45	1.79
	(1.658)	(.001)	(1.000)	(.800)	(1.444)	(.400)	(.500)
60) AB Recip	1.355	1.485	1.616	1.025	2.360	1.160	1.024
	(.771)	(1.000)	(1.188)	(.718)	(1.055)	(.250)	(.700)
61) APTD Recip	8.212	7.567	.526	8.594	7.926	5.976	4.359
	(.717)	(.631)	(.635)	(.775)	(.340)	(.717)	(.500)

**** Variables 58–61 show the relative *incidence* of recipients in each region, not the average percentage of recipients.

uniform in their political traits than is the nation as a whole; in the case of every dependent variable, most of the regions show smaller coefficients of variability than does the aggregate of 48 states. Moreover, for only ten of the 61 variables do more than one-third of the regions show greater diffusion (relative to their means) than does the nation as a whole. The large majority of our regions shows a degree of internal consistency suggestive of viable regional processes at work in the determination of political forms, processes, and politics. Yet this consistency is not similar from one region or one dimension of politics to the next. After we identify the gross differences that exist between the major regions of the country, we shall re-examine the coefficients of variability in order to identify those areas and dimensions of public affairs that show the greatest regional homogeneity.

NO-CENTRAL	UPP MID-WEST	BORDER	SO-EAST	SOUTH	CONFED	SO-WEST	MOUNTNS	FAR WEST	TRANS-PLAINS	TRANS-MISS
88.02	88.03	75.15	67.39	68.69	66.46	57.70	73.00	84.38	73.24	75.92
(.088)	(.082)	(.150)	(.193)	(.179)	(.186)	(.225)	(.224)	(.161)	(.252)	(.203)
4190.00	4340.00	4250.00	3710.00	3880.00	3710.00	3160.00	3090.00	3590.00	3180.00	3440.00
(.205)	(.157)	(.167)	(.096)	(.147)	(.097)	(.250)	(.233)	(.337)	(.286)	(.235)
142.82	160.50	112.70	79.10	87.41	74.42	118.03	143.22	144.33	141.23	136.79
(.211)	(.093)	(.170)	(.304)	(.323)	(.284)	(.220)	(.067)	(.173)	(.115)	(.169)
86.30	94.94	66.53	58.42	62.36	60.37	76.29	79.86	91.20	82.48	83.91
(.132)	(.137)	(.223)	(.208)	(.220)	(.209)	(.166)	(.189)	(.117)	(.171)	(.159)
89.03	96.18	74.56	60.53	66.00	61.70	87.63	82.47	107.21	91.60	90.80
(.156)	(.148)	(.299)	(.208)	(.267)	(.202)	(.245)	(.145)	(.146)	(.191)	(.197)
88.24	98.47	72.36	56.87	61.69	56.41	80.55	71.22	64.50	70.34	75.18
(.204)	(.256)	(.257)	(.200)	(.257)	(.185)	(.268)	(.141)	(.742)	(.399)	(.328)
1.20	1.19	1.84	1.06	1.20	.8635	1.68	1.68	2.54	2.12	1.59
(.425)	(.403)	(.348)	(.541)	(.558)	(.372)	(.542)	(1.132)	(.236)	(.344)	(.521)
1.24	1.51	1.58	1.32	1.44	1.33	3.39	6.93	8.17	7.04	4.67
(1.000)	(1.000)	(.500)	(.615)	(1.000)	(1.000)	(.667)	(.571)	(1.750)	(1.143)	(1.362)
1.081	.763	1.546	1.250	1.309	1.278	1.412	.877	2.271	1.506	1.314
(.545)	(.375)	(.563)	(.296)	(.385)	(.308)	(.357)	(.333)	(.652)	(.733)	(.702)
5.033	4.489	7.229	7.152	7.038	6.980	7.153	13.8	14.8	13.2	9.364
(.620)	(.289)	(.375)	(.326)	(.400)	(.400)	(.542)	(.565)	(.824)	(.664)	(.842)

Major Regional Patterns

In order to depict the gross differences between three major sections of the country, we can examine the regional groupings of demarcation 1, described in Chapter 2. The regions of that demarcation—North, Southeast, and Transmississippi—approximate the areas that are often called "North," "South," and "West." As it is expected, the Southeast scores on the low end of most measures. The Southeast is considerably below the national averages in most measures of voter turnout, two-party competition, the equity of legislative apportionment, the compensation of legislators and administrators, government expenditures and taxes, and many aspects of policy in the fields of education, highways, and welfare. However, there are some notable exceptions in the status of Southern politics and public policies. In the expenditures of state governments for education and welfare, and in state government tax effort, the Southeast scores above the North. These findings reflect the relative "centralization" of Southern state governments, which is also revealed in the high score of the Southeast on the percentage of state and local government revenue allocated to state agencies. Also, the state legislatures of the Southeast are larger and more active than those in Transmississippi; this reflects the importance of state institutions in Southern government and the preoccupation of Southern legislators with "local bills" that pertain to the affairs of a single community. The low score of the Southeast on property tax collections also signals the relatively small role assigned to localities. State governments in the region compensate for poor local efforts in public finance by their heavy use of the state-collected tax on retail sales. Finally, the Southeast scores high on the receipt of federal aids by state and local governments. Consistent with this is the high score of the region on several measures of educational programs that are supported with federal money: school lunches, vocational education, and vocational rehabilitation. Yet the high scores on these educational programs are not sufficient to compensate for other weaknesses in Southern education; the Southeast scores far below the national averages in the percentage of high school pupils who remain to graduate, and in the percentage of candidates who pass the nationwide mental examination.

On a number of traits, the primary regional distinctions appear between the Southeast and the remainder of the country; in these areas the North and Transmississippi score similarly and at opposite poles from the Southeast. The Northern and Western regions are equally high on voter turnout and party competition, the compensation of government employees, the use of property taxation, and service levels in the fields of education and welfare.

The North stands apart from the other major regions with high scores on the equity of legislative apportionment and low scores on several traits that measure the prominence of state (as opposed to local) authorities. State government expenditures and tax effort are low in the North, there is relatively little use of the sales tax, and a small percentage of state and local revenues is allocated to state agencies. Northern states also are low users of federal aid; they show a disinclination toward heavy investments in road mileage but have enviable records of highway safety. The contrary scores on highway mileage and safety may reflect the tendency of northerners to rely less than other citizens on highway transportation.

The Transmississippi region stands out with high government spending and tax effort, high use of federal aids, and extensive services in the highway field. Low scores on highway safety coexist with high scores on highway mileage. The product of the auto-truck transportation emphasis in the West is much road mileage and many highway deaths.

Secondary Regional Patterns

Once the gross differences between North, South, and West are evident, it is still necessary to examine our smaller regions and those which combine "border" states in various ways. All of the major sections contain smaller groupings within themselves that may show certain political traits in a highly distinctive fashion. And around the edges of the major regions there are some ambiguous border areas which may fit more uniformly in one major region or another, or which may be distinct regions in themselves.

In this intensive analysis of regional differences, we find the same lack of consistency from trait to trait that marked our examination of the three principal regions. Certain regional borders surround states that score distinctively on some aspects of politics but not on others. The discussion that follows does not produce one simple map of the United States showing "the most distinctive" or "the most salient" regional borders. Rather, the product will be a multi-faceted description of boundaries that vary in their saliency with the issue at hand.

In order to sort out the meaningful regional boundaries in the northeastern section of the country, it is necessary to examine means and coefficients of variability for the New England, Middle Atlantic, Great Lakes, Northeast, and North regions. Recall from Chapter 2 that New England, Middle Atlantic, and Great Lakes are each separable components of North, and that Northeast represents a slightly different grouping that combines New England and three of the five Middle Atlantic states: New York, New Jersey, and Pennsylvania. On the measures of voter turnout none of the smaller regions is more distinctive or differs markedly from the most inclusive of the regions (North). Indeed, this same finding is apparent for New England and Middle Atlantic on most of the dependent variables: their coefficients of variability are generally no smaller than those of the more inclusive regions. The exceptions to these findings occur in the variables that measure the regions' use of various taxes. New England scores higher and more consistently as a user of the property tax, and the Middle Atlantic region is more distinctive in its use of individual income taxes, current service charges, and government borrowing. Moreover, the Middle Atlantic states are distinctive in making low use of federal aids and having high recipient rates for the public assistance programs that aid families of dependent children and the disabled.

More than any other region in the greater North, the Great Lakes warrant consideration as a distinct entity. Their coefficients of variability are smaller than those of the North on most dependent variables, indicating greater uniformity within the Lakes region than within the larger region. The Lake states tend to show more intense party competition than the North as a whole; slightly more equity in the apportionment of their legislatures; smaller and less active (but better paid) legislatures; a better paid corps of government employees, but one that is smaller relative to state populations and less subject to the protections of a state merit system; lower expenditures by state governments, but a greater emphasis on locally collected and spent revenues; revenue systems that rely heavily on general sales taxes and relatively little on excises, individual income taxes, and government borrowing; an extensive (and largely paved) rural highway system; and a quickly developed interstate highway system.

In the western portion of the Northern region, two borders —one between Northeast and Northcentral and another surrounding the Upper Middle West—should be examined for their saliency. The Northcentral region extends from the outer border of the Northeast (on the Pennsylvania-Ohio line) westward to include the Dakotas, Nebraska, and Kansas. The Upper Middle West includes two states from the North (Michigan and Wisconsin) and two others from the Plains (Minnesota and North Dakota).

The states of the Upper Middle West show considerable uniformity, as well as distinctiveness from both the Northeast and Northcentral regions, on several traits. Compared to the other regions in the area, these states have more government employees and pay them higher salaries; they also show higher government expenditures and tax effort, a greater inclination to assign financial responsibilities to local (as opposed to state) governments, high levels of service in the field of education, and more generous public welfare payments. It is on these dimensions that the Upper Middle West earns its reputation for progressive government and public service. When the Northeast and Northcentral are examined together, the states of the Northeast stand out with greater expenditures, a greater use of individual income taxes, and more generous welfare payments. The Northcentral states show a greater orientation toward local (as opposed to state) administration, and higher scores on the measures of educational service.

In the southern part of the United States it is necessary to sort out the regional groupings labeled South, Southeast, Confederacy, Border States, and Southwest. In the discussion that follows, we shall test for the distinctiveness of the Southeast and Confederacy with respect to the greater South of which they are a part, and we shall compare the character of the Border States and Southwest with both the Southern and non-Southern regions with which they overlap. Among other things, we shall consider John Fenton's hypothesis that the Border States fall between the South and Middle West in their present stage of political development, and we shall attempt to determine if the Southwest is more like the South of the Old Confederacy, or like the states of the Plains, Mountains, or Far Western regions.

The distinction between the Confederacy and Border

States is clear on several dimensions of politics, especially those considered by John Fenton in *Politics in the Border States*. On the measures of voter turnout and party competition, the Border and Confederacy regions are both more uniform than the larger South, and they score predictably "progressive" and "conservative" on these two dimensions. The Border States score lower on turnout and competition than the non-Southern regions, but they score appreciably higher than do the states of the deeper South. They are also ahead of the Confederacy in the salary of government employees, the coverage of state merit systems, government expenditures, the use of individual income taxes, motor vehicle taxes and government borrowing, the success of academic programs, and the generosity of public welfare programs. In most of these traits the Border States and the Confederacy show lower coefficients of variability than the greater South; therefore their traits are more uniform and at the same time different from those of the greater South. In other respects, however, the Border and Confederacy regions are no more uniform in their own traits than is the more inclusive South. The two regions are not distinct from one another on the variables pertaining to the equity of legislative apportionment, the size, activism, or salary of state legislatures, or the distribution of responsibilities to state or local governments.

On several traits it is possible to construct a three-tiered map that shades from the Confederacy in the deep South, through the Border States, and finally to the North. As one goes further north on this map one finds increasingly progressive levels of voter turnout, two-party competition, state and local government spending, certain welfare payments, and success in academic programs. These findings support the Fenton hypothesis of progressive Southern exposure to Northern values. On other characteristics, however, there is no clear progression from south to north. The Border States score higher than the North on certain types of road mileage relative to population and the coverage of certain public welfare programs. On these traits the regions of the upper South and the North adhere to the characteristics that have emerged from their separate histories. The findings lend some weight to

Daniel J. Elazar's view of the geology of American political history: he sees regional traits formed by east-to-west migrations, rather than (as Fenton) the progressive exposure of south to north. Here, perhaps, the Fenton hypothesis of south-to-north progression has run afoul of the east-to-west strata.[1]

On the western perimeter of the South, the Southwest shows traits that intervene between the Confederacy and the Mountain and Far Western regions. Moreover, the coefficients of variability for the Southwest are sufficiently low—relative to neighboring groups of states—to warrant its being considered as a separate region. The Southwest most clearly plays the regional "middleman" on voter turnout; inter-party competition; the salary, size, and merit-system coverage of government employees; government expenditures; the use of property taxes, motor vehicle taxes, and current service charges; and the success of academic programs. These findings suggest an east-west geology of political forms and processes. Southerners carried many traits with them from the Southeast to the Southwest, but their traditions became diluted in the presence of immigrants from various sections of the country. On other dimensions of politics and policy, however, the Southwest has developed traits that do not fit the pattern of intervening between Southern and Western practices. Legislative apportionment was less equitable in the Southwest than in any other region of the country prior to *Baker* v. *Carr,* and on some aspects of public welfare activities the Southwestern states score higher than both western and southern regions. Like other sections of the country, the Southwest does not present a clear image in comparison to its neighbors; it presents instead the results of various historical pressures on a group of contiguous states.

The western regions also fail to present a distinct set of borders. There is a meaningful regional boundary separating the Plains and Mountain regions as concerns certain traits,

[1] See John H. Fenton, *Politics in the Border States* (New Orleans: Hauser Press, 1957); and Daniel J. Elazar, *American Federalism: A View from the States* (New York: Thomas Y. Crowell, 1966); the Fenton-Elazar controversy is discussed in Appendix A.

but on other traits these regions appear to be one aggregate. The same general finding prevails for the boundary between the Mountain and Far Western regions. And it makes sense to speak of certain traits shown by the Transmississippi region, because on those traits there are no salient divisions among any of the smaller groupings within the inclusive area.

Perhaps the sharpest difference within Transmississippi occurs between the Plains and Mountain regions. The Mountain region scores higher on voter turnout and several measures of party competition than the Plains, as well as on government salaries, expenditures, tax effort, and some measures of service in the fields of education, highways, and public welfare. Also, the Mountain states assign a larger proportion of governmental responsibilities to state (as opposed to local) authorities. However, on such service indicators as high-school completion, urban roads, progress on the interstate highway system, the incidence of paved rural roads, highway safety, and several welfare programs, the Plains are ahead of the Mountain states.

The boundary between the Mountain and Far Western regions is less sharp than that between the Plains and the Mountain region. The Mountain states show higher levels of voter turnout and of state and local government tax effort, as well as a greater reliance on federal aid, than the Far Western region, but on most other dimensions the two regions do not show clear differences. On the measures of party competition and the service indicators for public welfare, highway and education programs, for example, the Mountains and Far West trade places as the most competitive, or the most generous providers of services from one dependent variable to the next. The lack of clear distinctiveness between Mountains and Far West suggests the utility of the Transplains grouping, which combines the Mountain and Far Western regions with New Mexico and Arizona. When it is compared to the larger Transmississippi region, however, Transplains shows the influence of the deviant Southwestern states. On many of the dependent variables the coefficients of variability reveal that there is greater spread about the regional average within Transplains than within Transmississippi as a whole.

The Most Distinctive Regions

Which regions of the United States are generally the most uniform in political traits? Which of our political measures do not lend themselves to uniform regional sharing? These are questions that lead us away from the standard, orderly description of North, South, and West, plus the sub-regions within each. Now we are asking about the groupings of states that seem to qualify as the more clearly "regional" of all. And we are looking to see if any characteristics of politics are less likely than others to be shared by regional partners. The answers to the first question will tell us if each of the regions featured in the literature of political science is highly distinctive; the answer to the second may tell us something about the factors that get in the way of regional likeness.

By a simple count of the coefficients of variability for each region that are less than 0.1 in magnitude, it is possible to identify those regions that show the highest distinctiveness on the dependent variables. The results, shown in Table 3–2,

TABLE 3–2. THE INCIDENCE OF HIGH INTRA-REGIONAL UNIFORMITY: NUMBER OF COEFFICIENTS OF VARIABILITY LESS THAN 0.1

North	7
Northeast	5
New England	7
Middle Atlantic	7
Great Lakes	14
Plains	7
North Central	8
Upper Middle West	15
Border States	7
Southeast	8
South	3
Old Confederacy	8
Southwest	9
Mountains	11
Far West	6
Transplains	5
Transmississippi	3

are not altogether in keeping with the expectations to be found in the literature. Some of the regions that have been the subject of the most intensive inquiries (New England, Confederacy, Transplains) show a *low* incidence of highly distinctive scores on the dependent variables.

The region that shows the larger number of highly distinctive characteristics is the Upper Middle West. This band of four states (Michigan, Wisconsin, Minnesota, and North Dakota) shows internal consistency on the traits of high voter turnout and intense party competition, high state and local government tax effort and expenditures (especially for education), high per capita payments for property taxes, a high proportion of taxation-expenditure responsibilities given to local governments, and generous welfare payments to families of dependent children.

The Great Lakes region also shows a high incidence of distinctive political and policy traits, and exhibits uniformity on the traits of high voter turnout and intense party competition, a well-paid but relatively small corps of state and local government employees, relatively high state and local government expenditures (especially for education), a strong emphasis on locally collected and spent government revenues, low reliance on federal aid, and a low incidence of unpaved roads. Compared to the Upper Middle West, the Great Lakes states show somewhat less voter turnout and party competition, a lower level of government spending, less reliance on federal aids and better (i.e., more paved) secondary roads.[2]

The Mountain states comprise a third highly distinctive region, one whose uniform traits include scores on voter turnout and party competition that are among the highest in the country, relatively high salaries for government employees, the highest state and local government tax effort, high scores on

[2] This comparison of the Upper Middle West and Great Lakes regions is not contrary to John Fenton's contentions about the policies of the more northerly and southerly of the "Middle Western" states. See his *Midwest Politics* (New York: Holt, Rinehart and Winston, 1966). But the high distinctiveness of the Upper Middle West—including a state (North Dakota) that Fenton omitted from the Middle West—calls into question his narrow definition of the region.

the success of academic programs, and a generous program for the families of dependent children. Many traits of the Mountain region are unusual for its generally low level of economic development; we shall return to this region for a more intensive examination in Chapter 6.

The smaller regions in the northeastern quadrant show the most instances of internal diffusion. In particular, New England, Middle Atlantic, and the region that combines most of their states (Northeast) show the most coefficients of variability that exceed the national coefficients. Both New England and the Middle Atlantic encompass states that show widely divergent traits. In New England the division runs along the northern border of Massachusetts. The states above that line have remained relatively rural, Protestant, Yankee, Republican, and poor, while the states of southern New England have shown great population and political shifts with the immigration of millions of settlers from Ireland, Great Britain, and southern and eastern Europe. These immigrants provided the raw labor for burgeoning industrialization during the late nineteenth and early twentieth centuries, and with their descendants they have shifted the balance of electoral power to urban Catholic Democrats. This diffusion of social and economic traits may provoke the diffusion apparent in politics and policy.

Within the Middle Atlantic region a major division runs along the historic Mason-Dixon line. Below this border Maryland and Delaware show the heritage of the antebellum South along with the urban-industrial congestion that warrants their membership in the East Coast megalopolis. Certain governmental forms of these states resemble those of the deep South: low local taxation and expenditures, and many administrative responsibilities assigned to state agencies. The result is that the Middle Atlantic is particularly diffuse on measures of taxes used, levels of state government spending, and state-local intergovernmental relations.

We can also use coefficients of variability to identify those aspects of politics that are not shared in a uniform way by regional partners. Where regional coefficients on a trait are

generally larger than the coefficient for the entire United
States, we know that regional partners are more widely diverse
—in relation to their numbers—than are the 48 states. Among
the dimensions of state politics that show the *least* uniformity
within regional lines are equity in legislative apportionment,
sales taxation, and state progress on the interstate highway
system. The finding of regional diffusion on the measures
of legislative apportionment complements previous findings
about the correlates of apportionment. Several writers have
considered this aspect of state politics in relation to economic
development, voter turnout, party competition, and levels of
government expenditure, revenues and public services.[3] For
the most part they have been disappointed in their attempts to
relate apportionment with other characteristics of the states.
And here we find that scores on apportionment are not consistent from one state to another within regions. The equity of
legislative apportionment in the years before *Baker* v. *Carr*
seems to have been determined by factors unconnected with
other features of politics, policy, or regional norms. Perhaps
the dated nature of apportionment schemes is responsible for
this finding. The equity in apportionment that prevailed in
the early 1960's was not simply the result of conscious policy.
In many states the malapportionment occurred as unplanned
population movements worked their influence on legislative
districts that were not easily changed.

The lack of regional consistency in sales taxation may represent the development of that tax base as one that is more
widely used by state governments than any other throughout
the United States. Since the time when Mississippi introduced
the tax as a poverty-proof revenue producer in 1932, 44 states
have adopted a general sales tax. In recent years Massachusetts, New Jersey, and New York broke with long anti-sales
tax commitments by adopting statewide levies, and represent

[3] See Herbert Jacob, "The Consequences of Malapportionment: A
Note of Caution," *Social Forces*, XLIII (1964), 256–261; Thomas R. Dye,
*Politics, Economics and the Public: Policy Outcomes in the American
States* (Chicago: Rand McNally, 1966); Richard I. Hofferbert, "The Rela-
tion Between Public Policy and Some Structural and Environmental Vari-
ables in the American States," *American Political Science Review*, LX
(March 1966), 73–82.

in their own actions the attractions that this source of revenue offers in the face of contrary traditions.

The aregional nature of interstate highway development may reflect the nationalizing power of a new federal aid program that enters the scene with the insurmountable temptation of several billion dollars to be shared on a 90-to-10 federal-state basis. It is true that some states have taken more rapid advantage of this program than others, but regional norms do not appear to be salient in their decision. Although there are federal programs whose use is conditioned by regional practices (e.g., aid to dependent children, school lunches, and vocational education), the generosity of the federal-state sharing formula in the interstate program, the amount of funds at issue, and the widespread popularity of good roads seem to have overridden whatever regional considerations might have been raised. An alternate explanation is that the *barriers* to the completion of each state's highways are not regional in character. These roads provide odd combinations of profit and dislocations to property owners, businesses, and individuals. Their objections to proposed routings may have similar effects from one region to the next in postponing construction.

Consistent Regional Scores in Categories of Variables

It is still to be determined if the regions score consistently on the several measures in each of the categories of politics and policy that are featured in Table 3–1. To facilitate this analysis, the table underscores those two regions that score highest and the two that score lowest on each variable. In few categories of politics and public policy do we find the same regions scoring consistently high or low from one variable to another. Moreover, it may be no accident that one of these is the turnout-competition dimension of state politics. This more than other aspects of politics has been the frequent subject of regional analysis. On these traits there are relatively clear regional borders around the states that have reputations for high and low scores. For the Southern regions Table 3–1 shows the very low scores on turnout and the high scores on one-party dominance of state politics that observers have long discussed. Also as expected, the Mountain states show the highest levels of voter turnout and the most intense two-party competition.

As soon as we leave the realm of turnout and competition, the complexity of political regions becomes starkly apparent. In the equity of legislative apportionment, the Southwest scores consistently low, but the Confederacy scores low only on some measures. Thus, there is no clear Southern pattern on apportionment, as there is on measures of turnout and competition. The Northeast and New England show the most equitable apportionment, a finding that hardly squares with the origin of the term "gerrymander" as a label for a contoured district in Massachusetts. In the measures pertaining to state legislatures, New England scores highest on the number of legislators, reflecting the practice of giving at least one representative to each town. But on measures of legislative activism (variables 14 and 15), the Middle Atlantic region stands out with the highest scores. And on the length of session and compensation it is the Great Lakes region that is prominent. The Mountain region shows some negative consistency on the legislative traits; it scores close to the bottom on the measures for size, activism, length of session, and compensation.

On the measures of state and local administrative agencies, the Far West stands out with high scores on salaries, administrative size, and the coverage of the personnel system. But the Great Lakes reveals that these traits need not vary together; it scores high on salary, in the middle range on size, and very low on the coverage of the personnel system.

The Far West and Mountain regions are the high spending areas of the United States. They show the highest scores on the measures of state spending, and nearly the highest on the combined measures of state and local government spending. It is consistent with the South's image of fiscal conservatism and poverty that its regions score lowest on the combined measure of state and local spending, but the Southern regions are not as low on the measures of *state government* spending. This finding is complemented by high scores for Southern regions on the measure of state tax effort, and on the centralization of taxing and spending at the state level. A prominent characteristic of Southern states is their tendency to administer activities at the state level that are the responsibility of local governments elsewhere.

On the measures of tax effort no region scores in the highest (or lowest) ranks on both *state* and *state-plus-local* tax effort. The Mountain and Upper Middle West regions show the greatest state and local tax effort, but each of these regions scores well down the list on the measure of state tax effort. The Southeast and Southwest score highest on that measure, reflecting in part the large proportion of governmental assignments given to state governments in those regions. The lowest scoring region on tax effort is the Border (state plus local), and the Plains and Northcentral (state). These three regions overlap one another at the confluence of the Ohio and Mississippi Rivers. Missouri is the one state that is located in each of these low-tax regions (Border, Northcentral, and Plains), and it scores predictably low on both state and state-plus-local tax effort.[4]

The measures of revenue per capita from specific sources show that states of different regions tend to distribute their revenue loads in peculiar combinations among the available devices. The Far West is the only region to score highest in per capita revenues received from several sources. The states in that region draw heavily on general sales, excise, and motor vehicle taxes, plus current charges and government borrowing. The New England and Upper Middle Western states show the highest per capita payments for property taxes, and residents in the Middle Atlantic states pay the most in individual income taxes. At the time of these measurements, states in the Northeast showed the clearest aversion to the general sales tax, but this finding might be outdated by recent enactments in Massachusetts, New York, and New Jersey. The low payments for property taxes in Southern regions reflect the emphasis on state-collected revenues in that part of the country: Southern states score relatively high on their per capita collections from general sales and excise taxes. The Plains and Mountain states score lowest on government indebtedness, in contrast with the

---

[4] On the measure of state tax effort and state-plus-local tax effort Missouri shows 3.8 and 7.8 percent of personal income allocated to governments, respectively; the comparable U.S. averages (48 states) are 5.1 and 9.5 percent.

high reliance on indebtedness shown by the Far Western states. These low scores testify to the marked policy differences that may separate neighboring regions that show considerable similarity on other dimensions.[5]

On the measures of education service there are some consistent patterns in regional scores on the variables that pertain to federally aided programs (school lunches, vocational rehabilitation, and vocational education). The poor Southern regions score high as users of the federal programs, while the relatively wealthy regions of Northeast, Middle Atlantic, Great Lakes, and Far West score lowest on these variables. As might be expected, the poor Southern regions score lowest on the academic measures of exam success and school completion. Yet the regions that score highest on academic variables are not clearly the best developed economically; the Mountains, Plains, and Upper Middle West owe their high scores on the academic measures to something other than an advanced economic development.[6]

On the measures of public welfare programs the Far Western region scores consistently high on several measures of average benefits and the incidence of recipients among relevant populations. Thus it qualifies as the most welfare-minded of the regions. The Upper Middle West tends to show high average benefits in keeping with its reputation for progressive public services, but fails to show commensurate generosity in its recipient rates; the Middle Atlantic scores high on recipient rates but not on average payments. The Southeast scores predictably low on average benefits, but does not show low scores on recipient rates.

Summary

As we warned in the introduction, this chapter has not provided a quick tour through well-demarcated regions of

[5] The Mountain and Far Western regions show considerable affinity on the measures of voter turnout, party competition, government spending, and tax effort.

[6] The Mountain states score lowest as a region on total personal income; the Mountains, Plains, and Upper Middle West score on the middle or lower ranges on all three measures of economic development.

American politics. Depending upon the measures of politics or public policies that we employ, we find a variety of borders, sometimes distinct and sometimes diffuse, between the 17 regional groupings. Despite the frequent lack of clarity, however, a number of findings do emerge from this chapter that should further the understanding of regional differences in state politics.

1. On the measures of state politics considered in this book, there is greater uniformity within regions than in the nation as a whole. Although these findings do not provide direct evidence about the existence of shared historical experiences or regional norms that govern the behavior of politicians, citizens, or public officials, they do suggest the existence of regional processes—processes which may include shared experiences and norms—at work upon the character of state affairs.

2. When the nation is divided into the three large regions of North, Southeast, and Transmississippi, we find that the Southeast lives up to expectations and scores at the extreme end of many characteristics. On voting, apportionment, political competition, and many aspects of government structure and policy, the Southeast is the least "progressive" of the major regions. Neither the North nor Transmississippi, however, is clearly the most progressive of American regions. They resemble each other on voting, competition, and several measures of taxation and service. And they trade places as more and less progressive on such traits as apportionment, government expenditures, and highway services.

3. Within the northeastern quadrant, the Great Lakes region shows the greatest distinctiveness. New England and Middle Atlantic show relatively little differentiation from the more inclusive region labeled North.

4. In the southern part of the country there are numerous distinguishing traits that set off the Border States, Confederacy, and Southwest from one another. Both the Border and the Southwest regions intervene politically as well as geographically between the deeper South and non-Southern states. The blending of the Southern traits into the Border States suggests some support for Fenton's view of south-north political evolution.

5. In the western section of the country, the Plains, Mountains, and Southwest stand out distinctively from their neighbors. However, their traits do not place them clearly on a continuum: they trade high and low scores on the dependent variables, and they will require a piece-by-piece inquiry when it comes time to explain distinctive regional characteristics.

6. The identification of most and least distinctive regions produced some surprises. The regions that show the most internal uniformity on our traits, the Upper Middle West and the Mountains, have received little systematic treatment in the literature. In contrast, New England is often cited as a political region with deep historical roots, but its members show a low incidence of uniformity on our measures of politics and public policy.

7. The traits that show relatively little uniformity within regional lines provide us with some clues about the factors that can get in the way of regional processes. The aregional nature of interstate highway completions may reflect the nationwide appeal that can be presented by a lucrative new federal grant-in-aid program; or it may reflect the similar problems of state officials across the country in settling local conflicts over highway routings and the dislocations that are inevitable with major development. The recent popularity of the sales tax as a state revenue device may account for its low incidence of regional uniformity. Since the 1930's most of the states have discovered the large sums that the sales tax can collect in tolerably small amounts. Even since 1962, when the data for this study were collected, three states in the "low sales tax" region (Massachusetts, New York, and New Jersey) broke with their traditions and adopted new statewide levies. The failure of regional partners to show similar levels of equity in their legislative apportionment may reflect the dated nature of many apportionments. Unlike other policies, an apportionment scheme (prior to *Baker* v. *Carr*) was not refurbished periodically. Instead, apportionments tended to remain fixed. Their equity may not represent a *policy* subject to regional norms as much as haphazard patterns of population growth and movement.

4

REGIONAL CHANGE IN
THE TWENTIETH CENTURY

Until now we have focused on regionalism at one point in time. Our data has come from the period between 1960 and 1962, and almost all of the literature that has guided our analysis was written during the most recent decade. In this chapter we shall look into the background of current regional characteristics. Although the scarcity of data limits the breadth of historical analysis, it is possible to examine some traits over a period of sixty years. The inquiry deals with a theme that is explicit in much of the literature about American regions: their assimilation into dominant national patterns.[1]

The "nationalization" of American politics is typically viewed as an aspect of larger developments that are producing an integrated national economy and culture. Presumably, a

[1] See, for example, V. O. Key, *Southern Politics in State and Nation* (New York: Alfred A. Knopf, 1949), p. 671 ff.; Morton Grodzins, *The American Federal System*, Daniel J. Elazar, ed. (Chicago: Rand McNally, 1966), pp. 379 ff.; and Frank Munger, *American State Politics: Readings for Comparative Analysis* (New York: Thomas Y. Crowell, 1966), pp. vii–viii.

number of activities reflect the growing nationalism at the same time that they further its development: the prominence of network programming on television, the absorption of locally owned newspapers into national chains, the assimilation of local industries by national corporations, the growing homogeneity of working conditions and consumer goods across the country, the development of national "labor markets" for many professions and skilled trades, and the increasing number of state and local government programs that receive funds and performance standards from federal agencies.

Yet, the nationalization of American politics and public policies is more often alleged than demonstrated: it is evident that the nationalizing process has not proceeded so far as to obliterate the regions. Those who perceive homogenization may exaggerate the speed, if not the direction, of political changes. The influence of regional historical experiences and the inclination of state and community leaders to acquire their tax and service norms from neighboring states may be powerful enough to resist the often-cited pressures for nationalizing.

An examination of one reputed nationalizing force—federal grants-in-aid—reveals that it actually contains opportunities for the further development of regional norms. State and local governments do not act as underlings who respond obediently to the temptations of Washington gold; rather, state officials and political leaders present their demands for increased aid to the federal Congress and help to write the performance standards that will govern program administration. Spokesmen for the states are familiar with the opportunities presented by the checks and balances of the national government. They can use an alliance with a congressional committee to obtain a concession from an agency, or else use an alliance with an administrative agency to win concessions from a congressional committee. No studies have found that state or local governments are losing powers generally by receiving federal grants. Federal programs usually support "new" activities and permit state agencies to provide services not previously supported with state funds, and the states share certain decisions in these new programs with federal administrators. If "power" is defined as the ability to control one's environment, then increased knowledge, technological ability, and economic resources permit federal *and* state governments to increase their power simultaneously. In their exercise of new discretions, state officials are guided not only by national norms, but also in large measure by the norms regional administrators have evolved out of the cultural environment and interstate contacts that guide many of their decisions. The result may be the evolution of new regional standards relevant to the federal programs. For example, the level of federally aided welfare payments made by Southern states is considerably lower than in other regions, and lower even than the Southern economy would lead one to expect. State officials in the South have tailored their welfare activities to the conservative "anti-welfare" views that prevail in that region.

This chapter shows that the politics and policies of American regions are becoming, in certain respects, more like those of other regions. Generally speaking, all states are showing an increase in both popular participation in politics and financial support for public services. However, the "underdeveloped" states are showing more progress than the "developed" ones, so that ranges between extreme regions are becoming smaller and all states are clustering more tightly around the national averages. Yet this nationalization is not occurring uniformly in all aspects of state politics: in some cases individual regions are not sharing in the general progress toward national patterns, and in most cases the members of individual regions are becoming more like their neighbors. Regional homogeneity is a product of the same forces that produce the nationalizing tendency. The common factor is the tendency of state officials to take policy cues from outside their borders—from Washington and from regional neighbors. The now-more-tightly-bound regional partners may generate norms that are capable of resisting further nationalizing.

Techniques

We shall use a number of simple tests to define various aspects of regional change. In order to determine if the regions are becoming more alike, we shall examine changes in the *range* between high- and low-scoring regions. The smaller that range becomes, the more it will appear that extreme regions are coming to approximate the national tendency. But in those cases where all states are showing increasing magnitude of a trait (such as government expenditures), the very size of the range may widen although its relative nature may diminish. In order to correct for the increasing magnitude of our variables, we shall divide the range by the national average; the ratio will provide, for each of the data-years, figures that will show relative changes in the spread of extreme regions.

In order to identify changes by individual regions over time we shall examine each region's raw score over several years, and each region's score calculated as a percentage of the national average. In this way we shall find instances of absolute and relative change, and identify those regions whose development appears to be most responsible for emerging national patterns.

We shall use coefficients of variability to chart the changes *within regions* over time, and thus help to explain how the findings of regional strength coexist with increasing national patterns. Partly because regional partners have become more homogeneous in their traits during this century (and more meaningful as sources of policy norms), we continue to find that region is a variable to be reckoned with in political analysis.

Unfortunately, most of the variables employed in Chapter 3 are not available over an extensive period of time. The present chapter depends on a small collection of seven variables measured at scattered points between 1902 and 1962. Although the findings cannot be taken with the confidence that would adhere to a large collection of indicators, the variables are sufficient for our principal claims: there is a growing similarity among the regions in several dimensions of politics and policy, but this development is not sufficient to destroy regional vitality.

The variables considered in this chapter include measures of voter turnout, party competition, and government expenditures. Specifically, they are:

1. Percentage of voting-age population voting in elections for U.S. Representative, 1938, 1942, 1946, 1952, 1958, and 1962.

2. Percentage of voting-age population voting in elections for state governor, 1948 (or 1946), 1952 (or 1950), 1958 (or 1956), and 1962 (or 1960).[2]

3. Percentage of seats held by major party in lower house of state legislature, 1948, 1958, and 1962.

4. Percentage of seats held by major party in upper house of state legislature, 1948, 1958, and 1962.

5. Percentage of votes received by winning candidate for governor, 1932 (or 1930), 1936 (or 1934), 1940 (or 1938), 1944 (or 1942), 1948 (or 1946), 1954 (or 1952), 1958 (or 1956), and 1962 (or 1960).

6. Total state government expenditures per capita,[3] 1903, 1913, 1918, 1924, 1929, 1939, 1942, 1947, 1952, 1957, and 1962.

7. Total state and local government expenditures per capita, 1902, 1932, 1942, 1957, and 1962.

Changes in Regional Patterns

As is evident from the data of Table 4–1, which show regional scores on each of the dependent variables, nearly all the regions show increasing political participation, competition, and government spending over the span of years considered in this chapter. It is also generally true that the regions are less spread apart on these measures of politics and public policy. The ratios of ranges to national averages (also shown on Table 4–1) have declined since the earliest year of record for most of the dependent variables.

The nationalizing of state politics and policies has not proceeded uniformly in all dimensions. The process has been most consistent in government expenditures, and least appar-

[2] Here and in variable 5 the year in parentheses is recorded when there was no gubernatorial election in the first year given.

[3] For the measures of government expenditure, the spending identified by the U.S. Census Bureau as "general expenditures" was recorded.

TABLE 4–1. REGIONAL MEANS, RANGES, AND RATIOS OF RANGES TO

Means

	U.S.	NORTH	NO-EAST	NEW ENG	MID ATL	GRT LAKES	PLAINS	NO-CENTRAL	UPP MID-WEST
U.S. Rep Turn *									
1962	47.0	55.4	56.4	57.7	51.4	56.7	54.2	55.3	58.1
1958	44.1	54.8	56.2	57.6	52.6	53.7	52.5	53.0	51.7
1952	61.0	70.6	70.3	70.7	69.4	71.7	69.1	70.2	70.1
1946	35.5	45.6	45.1	44.8	44.1	48.1	41.8	44.4	43.1
1942	35.1	44.9	45.5	45.8	42.6	46.0	43.9	44.8	42.7
1938	46.2	58.3	60.6	61.7	56.2	56.2	59.7	58.3	54.6
Gov Turn									
1962	52.7	59.8	58.3	59.3	56.6	63.5	59.4	61.1	60.2
1956/58	49.9	59.4	57.8	59.1	56.2	63.0	57.1	59.6	57.2
1950/52	55.7	66.4	63.2	69.4	55.5	73.7	72.3	72.9	73.3
1946/48	39.7	48.8	46.0	45.6	48.1	53.5	46.3	49.3	45.9
Lower House Comp									
1962	70.3	62.8	64.1	68.9	62.9	55.4	63.7	60.3	54.3
1958	72.3	63.7	62.0	64.4	68.1	58.3	57.5	57.8	54.7
1948	79.9	76.0	73.8	73.1	73.0	82.4	80.1	81.0	83.8
Upper House Comp									
1962	72.8	65.2	66.9	69.9	63.4	61.5	66.0	64.1	65.7
1958	73.5	64.0	63.5	67.5	64.3	59.7	64.2	62.3	61.3
1948	80.0	75.3	74.3	75.1	69.0	81.7	80.5	81.0	80.5
Gov Comp									
1960/62	57.7	52.9	52.4	52.1	53.3	53.3	53.2	53.3	50.5
1956/58	62.3	54.4	53.9	54.0	55.3	54.0	53.6	53.8	54.3

* The complete title of each variable is shown in Chapter 2, pp. 34–41.

NATIONAL AVERAGES, 1902–1962

BORDER	SO-EAST	SOUTH	CONFED	SO-WEST	MOUNTNS	FAR WEST	TRANS-PLAINS	TRANS-MISS	Range	Range/National Average
46.2	25.8	29.7	22.2	40.1	61.3	52.9	55.3	52.9	39.1	.834
43.8	17.6	22.3	12.5	34.3	60.8	54.9	56.1	51.4	48.3	1.095
67.9	35.5	41.8	30.3	56.9	75.9	70.0	71.1	68.5	45.6	.748
40.0	14.7	19.0	9.5	26.2	48.3	39.5	41.9	39.8	38.8	1.093
34.5	11.3	15.4	7.1	25.6	49.0	43.7	44.5	41.5	41.9	1.194
47.1	16.4	21.7	10.4	35.0	61.8	55.3	56.9	54.4	51.4	1.113
60.2	35.2	38.3	29.4	42.4	65.8	59.1	59.8	57.6	36.4	.692
56.2	27.0	30.8	20.2	37.8	65.7	60.2	60.6	56.0	45.5	.912
59.4	28.0	34.4	24.1	53.8	63.3	59.9	62.1	63.9	49.6	.890
50.2	19.7	23.8	12.8	27.4	54.6	44.8	47.0	44.3	41.8	1.055
71.9	90.0	87.8	94.2	79.5	59.4	57.1	60.8	64.5	39.9	.568
82.8	94.7	93.5	97.4	87.8	62.5	62.7	85.7	65.8	42.7	.591
69.9	91.3	88.5	96.5	83.3	69.9	70.2	71.2	76.2	26.6	.332
66.2	90.7	88.1	96.7	89.9	56.6	63.9	64.7	68.0	40.1	.551
79.1	93.7	92.0	97.6	91.1	60.9	65.3	67.0	69.0	37.9	.516
68.0	92.7	89.1	97.6	90.3	68.2	64.1	70.2	76.1	33.5	.419
54.2	68.8	65.2	70.5	54.3	54.7	56.1	55.0	54.4	20.0	.348
59.8	81.2	78.6	86.4	68.1	53.5	57.5	54.8	57.2	32.9	.528

Table 4–1 (Continued)

Means

	U.S.	NORTH	NO-EAST	NEW ENG	MID ATL	GRT LAKES	PLAINS	NO-CENTRAL	UPP MID-WEST
Gov Comp (Continued)									
1951/54	62.1	53.6	52.8	53.1	52.6	55.3	60.9	58.6	61.6
1946/48	65.1	58.1	60.0	61.2	56.2	56.3	61.2	59.2	62.0
1942/44	64.6	56.3	59.0	60.4	54.4	53.3	59.7	57.0	53.4
1938/40	63.7	54.3	54.9	56.3	53.1	52.9	53.6	53.3	55.3
1934/36	63.6	53.1	54.1	54.1	53.7	51.3	55.9	54.0	52.4
1930/32	62.9	57.3	56.7	56.1	57.0	59.0	59.9	59.5	66.4
Total State Expend									
1962	181.40	168.70	168.70	179.59	172.33	154.27	166.89	161.45	190.46
1957	136.64	129.81	129.81	142.11	131.17	116.36	128.44	121.61	139.57
1952	98.31	89.46	81.62	83.56	102.24	82.58	92.41	88.48	106.08
1947	63.09	61.20	64.98	68.14	58.04	56.78	53.63	54.89	63.84
1942	36.93	36.93	36.93	38.04	38.04	35.08	34.71	34.71	39.22
1939	27.34	30.35	30.35	30.35	31.44	28.98	24.33	26.25	30.83
1929	20.61	21.43	22.88	24.73	23.08	15.57	20.61	18.55	19.82
1924	9.88	10.28	10.67	11.07	11.16	8.60	11.26	10.18	10.67
1918	5.23	5.81	6.49	7.17	5.13	4.92	5.02	4.97	6.81
1913	3.68	4.23	4.60	4.89	4.34	3.28	3.42	3.35	4.77
1903	2.24	2.46	2.87	3.05	2.31	1.97	1.97	1.95	2.45
Total State & Local Expend									
1962	320.10	326.10	328.90	328.00	329.40	320.60	325.90	323.70	360.10
1957	236.08	244.00	250.81	254.66	242.62	232.61	238.30	235.93	255.25
1942	68.74	74.73	79.52	76.42	77.13	70.30	69.74	69.98	77.26
1932	46.64	53.32	55.78	50.11	59.81	50.67	45.44	47.62	54.48
1902	1.89	1.73	1.67	1.58	1.59	2.04	2.33	2.21	2.44

BORDER	SO-EAST	SOUTH	CONFED	SO-WEST	MOUNTNS	FAR WEST	TRANS-PLAINS	TRANS-MISS	Range	Range/National Average
54.0	78.3	75.2	84.6	67.7	53.6	54.9	54.7	59.2	32.0	.515
55.4	81.0	76.5	86.2	64.1	54.4	67.2	59.4	61.3	31.8	.488
51.9	82.9	78.0	89.7	69.1	52.9	61.9	58.2	60.3	37.8	.576
57.2	85.1	81.2	91.5	73.0	55.4	56.0	56.8	58.4	38.6	.606
56.2	84.6	79.8	90.7	67.5	56.4	61.5	58.3	59.5	39.4	.619
56.6	76.3	72.9	80.7	61.0	55.3	62.1	57.2	59.4	25.4	.404
193.34	166.89	174.14	159.31	195.91	214.05	241.54	224.94	199.54	87.27	.481
135.69	118.88	127.08	119.99	161.24	157.14	184.19	172.17	153.04	67.83	.496
109.19	86.51	95.36	85.45	115.02	116.01	141.82	126.82	113.06	65.74	.613
54.65	51.60	53.00	51.29	74.45	77.60	91.98	85.80	71.29	40.69	.645
35.26	27.82	29.54	26.62	41.36	46.53	51.25	49.12	42.10	24.63	.667
26.28	18.30	21.05	17.97	28.71	33.90	38.56	35.27	30.35	20.59	.753
22.76	15.87	17.31	16.10	21.02	22.88	28.80	25.76	22.88	13.23	.656
8.46	5.84	6.82	5.99	9.48	11.36	16.16	13.24	11.95	10.32	1.045
3.91	2.95	3.29	2.99	5.75	7.32	6.99	7.22	6.12	4.04	.772
3.12	2.26	2.58	2.26	2.91	4.78	5.63	4.86	4.08	3.37	.916
1.59	1.37	1.46	1.36	1.72	2.91	4.09	3.18	2.60	2.73	1.219
295.00	255.60	268.00	253.50	311.40	372.00	423.50	384.90	354.10	167.90	.525
206.35	179.36	193.03	186.11	250.93	271.39	311.70	286.83	263.78	132.34	.561
55.77	43.58	47.32	43.23	62.58	86.24	102.77	89.73	79.04	59.54	.866
37.02	26.48	30.09	26.73	41.19	62.71	67.91	62.18	53.40	41.43	.888
1.14	.63	.78	.63	1.73	3.48	3.75	3.35	2.78	3.12	1.651

TABLE 4–2. REGIONAL MEANS AS PERCENTAGES OF NATIONAL AVERAGES, 1902–1962

	NORTH	NOEAST	NEW ENG	MID ATL	GRT LAKES	PLAINS	NO-CENTRAL
U.S. Rep Turn *							
1962	118	120	123	109	121	115	118
1958	124	127	131	119	122	119	120
1952	116	115	116	114	118	113	115
1946	128	127	126	124	135	118	125
1942	128	130	130	121	131	125	128
1938	126	131	134	122	122	129	126
Gov Turn							
1962	113	111	113	107	120	113	116
1956/58	119	116	118	113	126	114	119
1950/52	119	113	125	100	132	130	131
1946/48	123	116	115	121	135	117	124
Lower House Comp							
1962	89	91	98	89	79	91	86
1958	88	86	89	94	81	80	80
1948	95	92	91	91	103	100	101
Upper House Comp							
1962	90	92	96	87	84	91	88
1958	87	86	92	87	81	87	85
1948	94	93	94	86	102	101	101
Gov Comp							
1960/62	92	91	91	93	93	93	93
1956/58	87	87	87	89	87	86	86
1951/54	86	85	86	85	89	98	94
1946/48	89	92	94	86	86	94	91
1942/44	87	91	93	84	83	92	88
1938/40	85	86	88	83	83	84	84

* The complete title of each variable is shown in Chapter 2, pp. 34–41.

UPP MID-WEST	BORDER	SO-EAST	SOUTH	CONFED	SO-WEST	MOUNTNS	FAR WEST	TRANS-PLAINS	TRANS-MISS
124	98	55	63	47	85	130	113	118	113
117	99	40	51	28	78	138	124	127	117
115	111	58	69	50	93	124	115	116	112
121	113	41	54	27	74	136	111	118	112
122	98	32	44	20	73	140	125	127	118
118	102	35	47	23	76	134	120	123	118
114	114	67	73	56	80	125	112	113	109
115	113	54	62	40	76	132	121	121	112
132	107	50	62	43	97	114	108	111	115
116	126	50	60	32	69	138	113	118	112
77	102	128	125	134	113	84	81	86	92
76	115	131	129	135	121	86	87	119	91
105	87	114	111	121	104	87	88	89	95
90	91	125	121	133	123	78	88	83	93
83	108	127	125	133	124	83	89	91	94
101	85	116	111	122	113	85	80	88	95
88	94	120	113	123	94	95	98	96	95
87	96	130	126	139	109	86	92	88	92
99	87	126	121	136	109	86	88	88	95
95	85	124	118	132	98	84	103	91	94
83	80	128	121	131	107	82	96	90	93
87	90	134	127	144	115	87	88	89	92

Table 4–2 (Continued)

	NORTH	NOEAST	NEW ENG	MID ATL	GRT LAKES	PLAINS	NO-CENTRAL
Gov Comp (Continued)							
1934/36	83	85	85	84	81	88	85
1930/32	91	90	89	91	84	95	95
Total State Expend							
1962	93	93	99	95	85	92	89
1957	95	95	104	96	85	94	89
1952	91	83	85	104	84	94	90
1947	97	103	108	92	90	85	87
1942	100	100	103	103	95	94	94
1939	111	111	111	115	106	89	96
1929	104	111	120	112	76	100	90
1924	104	108	112	113	87	114	103
1918	111	124	137	98	94	96	95
1913	115	125	133	118	89	93	91
1903	110	128	136	103	88	88	87
Total State-Local Expend							
1962	102	103	102	103	100	102	101
1957	103	106	108	103	99	101	100
1942	109	116	110	112	101	101	101
1932	113	119	106	128	109	96	102
1902	92	88	84	84	108	123	117

ent in party competition.[4] The regional spread in measures of competition for state legislatures was *greater* in 1962 than during the first year of record. There has been little change in the status of the least competitive regions on this measure. During 1948–1962, Democratic strength in the legislatures of the Confederacy declined by only 2.3 percent in the lower houses,

[4] The ratios of ranges to national averages have decreased most evenly in the measures of government expenditures per capita; the ratios for 1962 are approximately one-third the magnitude of the ratios for 1902–1903.

UPP MID-WEST	BORDER	SO-EAST	SOUTH	CONFED	SO-WEST	MOUNTNS	FAR WEST	TRANS-PLAINS	TRANS-MISS
82	88	133	78	143	106	89	97	92	94
106	90	121	116	128	97	88	99	91	94
105	107	92	96	88	108	118	133	124	110
102	99	87	93	88	118	115	135	126	112
108	111	88	97	87	117	118	144	129	115
102	87	82	84	81	118	123	146	136	113
105	95	75	80	73	112	126	139	133	114
115	96	67	77	67	105	124	141	129	111
95	110	77	84	76	102	111	140	125	111
108	86	59	69	61	96	115	164	134	121
131	75	56	63	58	110	140	140	138	117
130	82	64	70	62	79	130	153	132	111
114	73	61	65	64	77	130	179	142	116
112	92	80	83	79	97	116	137	120	111
108	87	76	82	79	106	115	132	121	112
111	81	64	68	62	91	125	149	130	114
115	79	55	64	57	87	134	145	132	113
129	60	33	41	33	92	184	198	177	147

and 0.9 percent in the upper. The regional spread in measures of voter turnout has declined since the first data of the 1930's, but the development has not been continuous. The election of 1952, for example, brought about a marked but temporary decrease in the spread between high and low turnout states, apparently reflecting the attraction of Eisenhower's candidacy in the South. (See Table 4–2).

In most of the dependent variables it is the development of Southern regions that accounts for the appearance of greater national similarity. While most states have shown increases in government spending and voter participation, these increases have been greatest in the South. In the case of voter participation in gubernatorial elections, the rate in the Confederacy increased by 130 percent between 1948 and 1962, while the national rates increased by only 33 percent. In state government expenditures the Confederacy's 1903–1962 increase was 11,614 percent, while the national rate was 7,998 percent. Likewise in the combined expenditures of state and local governments: the Confederacy's score increased by 40,138 percent between 1902 and 1962 and the nationwide rate increased by only 15,837 percent.[5] None of these Southern developments is a product of the most recent years. In state government expenditures the Confederacy reached a level that was 76 percent of the national average as early as 1929 (as shown in Table 4–2), but the region's progress was set back during the Depression. In an early war year (1942) the region had returned to 73 percent of the national average and then spurted to 81 percent by 1947. By 1962, state expenditures in the Confederacy had moved little (relative to the national average) beyond their level of 1947. In the case of voter turnout, the Confederacy in 1962 was not substantially above a level reached in 1952. Participation in congressional elections was 50 percent of the national average in 1952 and it was only 56 percent of the national average during the gubernatorial elections of 1960/1962. When the region's turnout is viewed in absolute data (Table 4–1), it is apparent that it did not regain the level of the 1952 election by 1962.

The lack of marked progress after 1952 in Southern turnout, competition, and government expenditures may reflect the holding power of regional norms in the face of economic development. During that period of little relative change in politics and policy, per capita personal income in the Confederacy increased by 68 percent (1950–1962) while the national increase was only 48 percent. It is possible that Southern levels of voter participation and government expenditures will go

[5] Note that these percentage figures for increasing government expenditures do not correct for inflation. See my *Spending in the American States* (Chicago: Rand McNally, 1968), Chapter V.

beyond the levels (relative to national averages) of 1962, but the change will probably not respond to economic development alone. It may take an active enforcement of federal civil rights legislation, plus active programs of citizenship training and generous grant-in-aid programs, to bring the South more into line with national trends in voter participation and government expenditures.

States in the Great Lakes and Upper Middle West have developed in the direction of more intense party competition, particularly in the state legislatures, where the regions have moved from 3–5 percent *less* competitive than the nation as a whole to 21–23 percent *more* competitive between 1948 and 1962. We may attribute this change to the interaction of three factors: developing industrialization, unionism, and refurbished Democratic parties. Industrial change attracted Southerners to the growing cities in the region, and these immigrants brought Democratic inclinations with them. The development of strong labor unions in Ohio, Michigan, Indiana, and Wisconsin rested upon this industrialization, and reinforced the Democratic tendencies that it provided. In Wisconsin, these processes were associated with a large base of sympathetic voters—the members of the declining Progressive party—who came to accept a Democratic affiliation.

Up to the time of World War II state governments in three of the northeastern regions (Northeast, New England, and Middle Atlantic) spent at levels ten to thirty percent above the national average. In more recent years, however, they have spent below the national average. Two explanations come to mind for this downward shift: it may reflect either the relative lack of innovation in government programs throughout the Northeast, or the continuing vitality of local governments. Local governments in New England, especially, have exercised considerable powers since Colonial days; the decline in state government expenditures might reflect innovations at the local level. However, the aggregate of state and local government expenditures has also declined (relative to national averages) in the northeastern regions since 1942. Thus, there appears to be a general tendency for governments in that section to fall behind nationwide rates of development. Although such states as Massachusetts and New York have long-established reputations as national leaders in certain aspects of public welfare, labor regulation, and high-speed limited access highways, these same states have recently suffered the problems of lengthy executive-legislative battles over new tax programs. Northeastern states in general rely heavily on real property taxes, and the unpopular nature of that levy may depress the governments' capacity to innovate.

State governments in the Southwest have shown a great advance in their expenditures during the century. Prior to World War I they spent at a level 20 percent below the national average, but within the last decade they have spent at a level 18 percent above the national average. One dramatic spurt came after 1913 with the maturation of new state governments in Oklahoma, New Mexico, and Arizona. The earlier spending figures of these states represent the budgets of territorial governments with small populations, but as populations and government structures increased in size, spending increased markedly. More recently, the Southwest made another spurt in state expenditures after 1939; this may reflect further changes in population, associated partly with the development of defense installations and (especially in Texas) defense-related industry.

Growth in Regional Uniformities

At the same time that regions are becoming more like one another, the member states within most regions are becoming more similar in their levels of political participation, competition, and government spending. This is evident in the data of Table 4–3, which show coefficients of variability for each of the dependent variables by region. In most cases coefficients for the most recent year (1962) are smaller than coefficients for the earliest years of record.

The finding of greater intra-regional uniformity suggests that regions are becoming more viable politically while they are becoming more like one another. Although it may seem paradoxical that there are simultaneous movements toward both greater regional similarity and greater national similarity, nothing in the nature of regionalizing or nationalizing precludes their common development. As we are using the terms in this analysis, they do not refer to mutually exclusive ideologies of national or regional loyalty; instead, they merely identify the sharing of regional or national patterns of political activity or public policy. The developments toward greater national and regional sharing reflect the common ingredient of an expanded field of vision. State officials and political elites are emulating their counterparts in other states more now than in the past, and this emulation has both regional and national manifestations.

Increasing national and regional sharing of traits may respond to the same underlying phenomena. Improved interstate communications and improved professional training for administrators produce greater attention to both regional and national "models" of politics and public policy. Associations of state (and local) government officials have national and regional meetings that provide important interstate communications. There were only two of these organizations before 1900, 19 by 1930, 37 by 1950, and 46 by 1966.[6] The development of these organizations and other communications media reflects the spread of federal aids from one field of service to another, and of federally sponsored programs of intergovernmental communications. However, such communications do not necessarily have a nationalizing impact. Federal officials have promoted the development of both regional and national associations for public officials in order to provide additional linkages between their own federal agencies and state and local governments. Federal agencies generally communicate with state and local officials through regional offices. The regional administration of federal grants may facilitate "adjustments" to local conditions, and foster the development of regional norms for each of the programs.

Because the officials of most state and local governments seem to have a regional orientation, it is not difficult to understand how an increase in interstate communications produces

6 Jack L. Walker, "The Adoption of Innovations by the American States," a paper delivered at the Annual Meeting of the American Political Science Association, Washington, 1968. Mimeo.

TABLE 4–3. REGIONAL COEFFICIENTS OF VARIABILITY, 1902–1962

	U.S.	NORTH	NO-EAST	NEW ENG	MID ATL	GRT LAKES	PLAINS	NO-CENTRAL
U.S. Rep Turn *								
1962	.330	.122	.102	.097	.164	.098	.137	.119
1958	.432	.127	.107	.103	.151	.111	.132	.132
1952	.311	.141	.171	.211	.143	.056	.058	.057
1946	.444	.196	.178	.222	.205	.167	.095	.136
1942	.514	.222	.022	.283	.186	.217	.091	.156
1938	.478	.138	.098	.097	.161	.179	.133	.156
Gov Turn								
1962	.321	.159	.103	.105	.198	.188	.136	.164
1956/58	.380	.136	.086	.102	.179	.143	.123	.133
1950/52	.411	.212	.238	.203	.304	.041	.028	.027
1946/48	.450	.245	.196	.239	.271	.222	.152	.204
Lower House Comp								
1962	.229	.167	.156	.123	.200	.091	.172	.167
1958	.250	.203	.145	.172	.250	.207	.123	.155
1948	.188	.158	.149	.192	.055	.183	.200	.185
Upper House Comp								
1962	.233	.143	.164	.149	.151	.097	.212	.172
1958	.230	.172	.156	.162	.234	.067	.172	.145
1948	.200	.133	.149	.160	.116	.085	.247	.185
Gov Comp								
1960/62	.204	.059	.059	.068	.043	.071	.056	.059
1956/58	.247	.074	.074	.089	.090	.047	.051	.047
1951/54	.245	.076	.079	.095	.036	.084	.165	.144
1946/48	.229	.117	.138	.166	.035	.074	.097	.095
1942/44	.254	.129	.142	.168	.057	.079	.133	.126
1938/40	.262	.073	.092	.101	.039	.038	.058	.050

* The complete title of each variable is shown in Chapter 2, pp. 34–41.

UPP MID-WEST	BORDER	SO-EAST	SOUTH	CONFED	SO-WEST	MOUNTNS	FAR WEST	TRANS-PLAINS	TRANS-MISS
.074	.216	.479	.465	.276	.229	.074	.072	.135	.181
.077	.295	.778	.818	.538	.588	.082	.036	.107	.255
.057	.162	.472	.476	.333	.246	.079	.071	.113	.145
.070	.225	.867	.842	.500	.500	.104	.175	.214	.250
.140	.314	1.091	1.000	.571	.500	.041	.182	.178	.262
.145	.277	1.000	.864	.600	.543	.048	.109	.140	.259
.083	.267	.540	.500	.414	.238	.106	.136	.167	.197
.105	.268	.778	.710	.700	.421	.121	.117	.148	.232
.027	.339	.821	.735	.792	.222	.286	.133	.194	.188
.065	.320	.950	.875	.692	.481	.236	.244	.277	.318
.093	.125	.138	.136	.085	.188	.102	.140	.148	.191
.055	.108	.084	.085	.052	.148	.111	.111	.152	.212
.214	.100	.143	.157	.052	.205	.086	.286	.183	.197
.167	.212	.165	.182	.062	.078	.088	.125	.185	.219
.066	.139	.106	.120	.151	.121	.098	.077	.179	.203
.185	.162	.129	.169	.051	.133	.147	.250	.214	.224
.014	.050	.278	.271	.272	.019	.027	.130	.076	.066
.037	.173	.215	.219	.156	.267	.062	.048	.064	.167
.203	.049	.237	.258	.185	.302	.052	.042	.053	.192
.075	.037	.205	.240	.157	.287	.034	.268	.199	.192
.056	.028	.221	.265	.138	.300	.062	.182	.158	.197
.063	.123	.195	.225	.114	.256	.067	.087	.108	.189

Table 4–3 (Continued)

	U.S.	NORTH	NO-EAST	NEW ENG	MID ATL	GRT LAKES	PLAINS	NO-CENTRAL
Gov Comp (Continued)								
1934/36	.259	.083	.071	.055	.086	.115	.066	.094
1930/32	.219	.109	.123	.141	.077	.109	.153	.131
Total State Expend								
1962	.23	.23	.23	.21	.29	.18	.18	.18
1957	.26	.25	.23	.18	.35	.21	.18	.19
1952	.28	.29	.06	.05	.42	.22	.20	.21
1947	.28	.18	.13	.11	.17	.24	.10	.17
1942	.27	.17	.13	.14	.24	.13	.15	.14
1939	.32	.20	.14	.06	.27	.26	.26	.27
1929	.41	.44	.41	.44	.45	.26	.38	.36
1924	.44	.25	.15	.15	.27	.30	.46	.43
1918	.43	.30	.31	.22	.26	.33	.34	.32
1913	.45	.29	.24	.24	.17	.38	.37	.35
1903	.50	.41	.41	.40	.16	.24	.29	.26
Total State-Local Expend								
1962	.192	.110	.121	.119	.140	.094	.121	.094
1957	.219	.145	.178	.181	.146	.091	.121	.106
1942	.292	.136	.131	.097	.207	.077	.149	.119
1932	.378	.265	.321	.329	.275	.152	.128	.144
1902	.672	.306	.341	.367	.371	.152	.373	.312

both greater regional and national similarities. As we suggested in Chapter 1, there may be a two-step communications process at work, with the elites of most states seeking to emulate the "leading states" within their region, and with the "regional leaders" either generating their own innovations, or taking their cues from leading states in other regions.

UPP MID-WEST	BORDER	SO-EAST	SOUTH	CONFED	SO-WEST	MOUNTNS	FAR WEST	TRANS-PLAINS	TRANS-MISS
.163	.062	.201	.242	.130	.296	.056	.110	.091	.167
.114	.048	.247	.248	.205	.217	.082	.153	.126	.150
.10	.18	.20	.21	.20	.22	.19	.11	.15	.21
.15	.33	.26	.29	.26	.28	.19	.14	.18	.24
.13	.38	.25	.33	.25	.25	.14	.11	.15	.23
.17	.25	.19	.22	.20	.35	.11	.27	.20	.30
.05	.29	.30	.31	.26	.32	.08	.15	.12	.23
.28	.35	.34	.39	.32	.20	.17	.18	.17	.26
.07	.54	.22	.40	.22	.33	.34	.47	.36	.38
.14	.48	.19	.42	.22	.36	.33	.43	.38	.43
.16	.26	.27	.31	.29	.52	.24	.41	.31	.37
.12	.48	.33	.44	.34	.43	.19	.55	.41	.46
.11	.37	.41	.41	.44	.50	.21	.38	.39	.75
.028	.100	.141	.148	.160	.129	.189	.095	.154	.172
.034	.214	.219	.220	.213	.135	.148	.137	.139	.163
.035	.188	.253	.257	.242	.217	.070	.082	.151	.220
.115	.282	.226	.314	.237	.333	.204	.268	.249	.296
.451	.289	.317	.436	.349	.520	.247	.573	.439	.496

Summary

In this chapter we have considered the alleged "nationalization" of politics and public policies in the United States. Our evidence both supports and modifies the common view: it is true that regions resemble each other more than in the past on measures of government expenditure, political participation, and party competition, but it is also true that regions themselves are becoming more uniform in these characteristics. Although our findings may be affected by the small number of indicators that are available, there appears to be a development toward both greater regionalism and greater nationalization—complementary movements which may seem odd in juxtaposition, but which show in common the tendency of elite groups within the states to look beyond their borders in search of norms. The product is both a reflection of the historic strength shown by regional identifications and an indication that regional norms remain viable in the face of pressures for common nationwide developments. When state elites feel inclined to look to other states for cues, they are most likely to initiate communications with regional partners. Perhaps only a few states act as inter-regional communications media, either by developing their own innovations and sending messages to states in other regions, or by adapting innovations from leading states in other regions. Because the communications of most states seem to be regionally oriented, the same federal programs that promote the nationalization of public policies may provoke the development of regional norms within the scope of each new federal venture.

5

ECONOMIC AND NON-ECONOMIC
EXPLANATIONS OF REGIONAL
PATTERNS

In Chapter 3, we took the first steps toward defining the regional character of American politics. Although the findings are obscured by regional borders that shift with the aspects of politics that are at issue, it is apparent that region is a variable worth considering in the political science of American states. Yet we have not faced the issue of economic influences over state politics. There is a good deal of evidence to suggest that economic conditions exert critical weight upon our dependent variables. A number of economists have found strong positive relationships between per capita state and local government expenditures and the economic characteristics of per capita personal income and urbanization; several political scientists have found sizable relationships between similar economic indicators and measures of voter turnout, inter-party competition, the professionalism of state legislatures, and public service levels in the fields of education, public welfare, and highways. These findings are reported further in Appendix A.

Populations that are relatively wealthy and urbanized tend to show high levels of voter turnout, intense party competition, well-paid and active state legislators, well-supported public education, and a generous level of payments to recipients of public assistance programs. The wealth and urban sophistication of these citizens may support the attitudes necessary for an acceptance of liberal access to the political process and competition between alternative approaches to policy making, and may provide the willingness and the economic substance for expensive programs in public education and welfare. In contrast, it is the less wealthy, rural states that spend the most on highways. As Dye speculates:

> . . . rural politics are much more highway-oriented than urban politics. Part of this phenomena may be a product of the historical problems of rural isolation; "Let's Get Out of the Mud" was a familiar battlecry in rural politics a few years ago. Rural roads disturb relatively few individuals, while a metropolitan highway involves uprooting thousands of outraged residents and irate businessmen. Freeways are only a good idea when they run through someone else's backyard! . . . [and] it may be that urban dwellers have come to accept traffic jams as facts of life: they have never known anything better, so they fail to fight for highways with quite the same zest as their country cousins.[1]

Insofar as economic conditions within the states may be the crucial determinants of state politics and public policies, this analysis of regionalism might produce nothing more than regional peculiarities that boil down to the characteristics determined by the tendency of regional partners to resemble one another economically. However, within each of the regions considered in this book there are considerable variations in economic status. Because of this, it *might not* be the economic characteristics of neighboring states that create similar traits of politics and policy.

The economic heterogeneity of American regions is evident

1 Thomas R. Dye, *Politics, Economics and the Public: Policy Outcomes in the American States* (Chicago: Rand McNally, 1966), p. 161.

TABLE 5–1. REGIONAL MEANS AND RANGES ON THREE ECONOMIC MEASURES

	PERSONAL INCOME/CAPITA		URBANIZATION		TOTAL PERSONAL INCOME	
	Mean	Range	Mean	Range	Mean	Range
North	$2538	$3102–1917	70.9%	88.6–38.5%	$14194	$50985– 782
Northeast	2504	3089–1917	71.3	88.6–38.5	13818	50985– 782
New England	2393	3089–1917	66.1	86.4–38.5	4743	14290– 782
Mid-Atlantic	2793	3102–2363	76.8	88.6–65.6	21184	50985–1455
Great Lakes	2457	2844–2283	70.7	80.7–62.4	18547	28857–9341
Plains	2229	2384–2065	53.0	66.6–35.2	5055	10362–1459
Northcentral	2324	2844–2065	60.4	80.7–35.2	10677	28857–1459
Upper Midwest	2302	2416–2236	58.4	73.4–35.2	9469	19307–1459
Border	2266	3102–1712	58.4	72.7–38.2	5588	10362–1455
Southeast	1699	2044–1285	50.0	74.0–37.7	5833	11158–2742
South	1880	3102–1285	54.8	75.0–37.7	6565	20361–1455
Confederacy	1716	2044–1285	53.8	75.0–37.7	7443	20361–2742
Southwest	1960	2097–1824	69.5	75.0–62.9	7512	20361–1860
Mountains	2153	2370–1941	60.6	74.9–47.5	2049	4520– 790
Far West	2749	3278–2333	71.8	86.4–62.2	15525	49181–1098
Transplains	2335	3278–1824	66.4	86.4–47.5	7033	49181– 790
Transmississippi	2260	3278–1824	62.0	86.4–35.2	6889	49181– 790
United States	2212	3278–1285	61.9	88.6–35.2	9060	50985– 782

from the comparison of regional means and ranges shown in Table 5–1. The ranges are sufficiently broad so that the scores of most regions overlap with those of other regions. The Southeast scores lowest on per capita personal income and urbanization. On the measure of per capita personal income, however, the *lowest* score in most of the non-Southern regions is lower than the highest score in the Southeast. On the other economic measures there is even greater overlap. On urbanization, all the regions have at least one state that is *less* urbanized than the most urban state of the Southeast. On total personal income (i.e., the aggregate of all personal income within each state, *not* corrected for population size), the Mountain region has the lowest average, but every region except one has at least one state with lower total personal income than the wealthiest state of the Mountain region. The diffusion of economic resources among the regions makes it unlikely that economics alone are responsible for the regional patterns apparent in state affairs. In many cases, regions are more homogeneous on measures of politics than on the measures of economic development.

The regional means on the economic measures, when considered in light of the findings in Chapter 3, testify further to the "slippage" between economic characteristics and our dependent variables. The best-developed region of America is the Middle Atlantic, which scores highest on each of the economic variables. Yet the Middle Atlantic is hardly mentioned among the regions showing the most "progressive" levels of turnout, competition, legislative apportionment, government expenditures, or public services. The Upper Middle West and Mountain regions place high on several measures of turnout, competition, spending, and services, but they place nowhere near the top on the economic measures. Moreover, the Mountain region scores below average on per capita personal income and urbanization, and lowest of all on total personal income. The Upper Middle West places below average on urbanization, and only slightly above average on per capita personal income and total personal income.

The most prominent case of extreme values on the measures of politics and policy that mirror themselves in the economic variables can be found in the low turnout, competition, and service scores of the Southern regions (South, Southeast, and Confederacy). Even here, however, we cannot tell from an inspection of Tables 3–1 and 5–1 whether the economic scores of Southern regions are commensurate with their scores on politics and public policy. It will require a sophisticated regression analysis to determine if Southern scores on economics and politics are actually in line with one another.

The principal task of this chapter is to identify the relationships between the economic and the political variables considered in this book, and to test the economic explanation for regional patterns of politics and public policy. First, we shall document the nature of the economic-political relationships that prevail over the country as a whole, specifying how much of the interstate variations in politics are explained by interstate variations in economic conditions, and how much of the variations in politics are left to be explained by other factors. Second, we shall evaluate the economic explanation for the regional uniformities that were discussed in Chapter 3. Out of this will come an understanding of which traits are best explained by current economic conditions and which must be explained by other regional characteristics.

Techniques

This chapter considers the relationships between the 61 measures of state politics employed in the previous chapter and three economic measures that assess the personal well-being, urbanization, and total economic resources within each state. The economic variables are (*a*) per capita personal income; (*b*) percentage of population living in urban areas; and (*c*) total personal income. These aspects of each state's economy tend to vary together, as indicated by their intercorrelations (product-moment) in Table 2–2. Thus, states with high average levels of personal well-being (*a*) also tend to show a relatively large percentage of their populations living in urban areas (*b*) and a large pool of available economic resources (*c*). However, these variables are not so tightly intercorrelated that we can predict a state's score on one economic measure simply by knowing its score on another measure. Thus, it appears that they assess distinct aspects of each state's economy and warrant consideration as separate influences on state politics and public policies.

The statistical tests to be used in this chapter reflect our recognition that the states' economies are not all of one piece. Rather than being content to determine the "economic" impact on politics, we go on to determine the differential importance of personal well-being, urbanization, and total economic resources. We employ coefficients of simple (product-moment) correlation to discern the relationship between each dependent variable and each economic measure, considered individually. For the purpose of discerning the relative weight of each economic measure while controlling for the influence of the others, we employ coefficients of partial correlation; thus we can determine which of the economic measures most frequently show relationships with the dependent variables that are independent of other economic measures. The coefficients of partial correlation provide evidence, therefore, about the economic characteristics that are generally most important with respect to state politics. Finally, coefficients of multiple determination (R^2) indicate the explanatory power of all three economic measures taken together with each dependent variable, and show the percentage of interstate variation in a measure of politics or public policy that is explained, statistically, by the aggregate of economic variables. For our purposes the coefficients of multiple determination also indicate the proportion of interstate variation that is *not* explained by economic conditions, and thereby highlight the explanatory power that may be left to other regional characteristics.

In our second principal analysis, the major statistical tool is analysis of covariance, whereby it is possible to depict relationships between an interval dependent variable (a measure of state politics) and interval and nominal independent variables (economic characteristics and region) while controlling successively for each likely influence. The correlation coefficients shown in Table 5–3 differ in conception from the product-moment relationships used in Table 5–2. We cannot use the coefficients in Table 5–3 to measure the proportion of variation explained by region and/or economic development, but we can use them with tests of significance to measure the relative prominence of economics or non-economic regional traits in the explanation of each dependent variable.[2]

It should be clear from the discussion in Chapter 3 that our findings may depend on which definitions of "regions" are employed. To permit the complex and diffuse nature of regional alignments to show itself, we shall perform three analyses of covariance, each with different groupings of the states. The first analysis uses the demarcation, described in Chapter 2, which divides the country into *North, Southeast,* and *Transmississippi.* The second analysis employs a demarcation that subdivides two major regions of the first grouping: the North becomes *New England, Middle Atlantic,* and *Great Lakes;* Transmississippi becomes the *Plains, Mountains, Southwest,* and *Far West;* and the *Southeast* remains as it is. The third analysis employs the principal regional divisions of the U.S. Census Bureau. As they are labeled here, the regions are *Northeast, Northcentral, South,* and *Transplains.* The demarcations employed in this chapter utilize fourteen of the seventeen regions defined in Chapter 2. For a list of the member states of each region, the reader may refer to Table 2–1 and Maps I, II, and III.

Economic Influences on State Politics and Public Policy

Over the nation as a whole, the measures of economic characteristics show consistent relationships with most measures of state politics and policy. The coefficients in Table 5–2 indicate that states with high levels of per capita personal income, urbanization, and total personal income tend to show high voter turnout, intense two-party competition, active and professional legislators, a large and well-paid corps of administrators, high state and local government revenues and expenditures per capita, and generous support for several aspects of education, highway, and public welfare services.

Perhaps when there are generally high levels of personal

2 Analysis of covariance receives additional treatment in the discussion of statistical techniques in Chapter 2. The procedures employed can be found in Hubert M. Blalock, *Social Statistics* (New York: McGraw Hill, 1959), Chapter 20; the computer program employed is "Analysis of Covariance with Multiple Covariates: BMD04V," in *BMD Biomedical Computer Programs* (Los Angeles: University of California, 1965), pp. 525–542.

TABLE 5–2. COEFFICIENTS OF SIMPLE CORRELATION, PARTIAL CORRELATION,† AND
MULTIPLE DETERMINATION BETWEEN THREE ECONOMIC MEASURES AND
THE DEPENDENT VARIABLES

	SIMPLE CORRELATION			PARTIAL CORRELATION			R^2
	income/ capita	*urban*	*total income*	*income/ capita*	*urban*	*total income*	
1) U.S. Rep Turn‡	.59***	.27	.08	.59***	−.15	−.17	.40*
2) Gov Turn	.52***	.21	.06	.54***	−.17	−.13	.33*
3) Lower House Comp	−.62***	−.38**	−.27	−.53***	.09	−.03	.39*
4) Upper House Comp	−.62***	−.38**	−.17	−.58***	.14	.07	.41*
5) U.S. Rep Comp	−.54***	−.34*	−.28*	−.45**	.10	−.09	.31*
6) Gov Comp	−.39**	−.25	−.12	−.31*	.01	.05	.15
7) Gov Tenure	−.40**	−.22	−.08	−.36*	.04	.08	.17*
8) Lower House Tenure	−.29*	−.24	−.19	−.17	−.04	−.05	.09
9) Upper House Tenure	−.25	−.24	−.05	−.13	−.13	−.12	.09
10) Schubert-Press	.08	.00	.06	.12	−.11	.07	.02
11) Dauer-Kelsay	−.24	−.28*	.07	−.09	−.28	.30*	.16*
12) David-Eisenberg	.34*	.26	.25	.22	−.01	.11	.13
13) Legislators	−.02	.04	.14	−.07	.00	.15	.03
14) Bills Intro	.36*	.45**	.68***	.04	.05	.58***	.47*
15) Bills Pass	.23	.34*	.60***	−.04	.02	.52***	.36**
16) Legis Session	.15	.25	.37**	−.05	.07	.29*	.14
17) Legis Compen	.47***	.56***	.79***	.12	.09	.69***	.64**
18) Employees Salary	.79***	.71***	.57***	.60***	.24	.30*	.71**
19) Employees	.35*	.14	−.08	.37*	−.04	−.24	.19*
20) Merit System	.20	.00	−.29*	.32*	−.02	−.39**	.22*
21) Total St Expend	.14	.14	−.26	.30*	−.11	−.29*	.15
22) St Educ Expend	.00	.03	−.11	−.02	.10	−.15	.02
23) St High Expend	−.03	−.39**	−.41**	.39**	−.40**	−.29*	.32**
24) St PW Expend	−.11	.09	−.01	−.24	.24	−.06	.07
25) Total SL Expend	.61***	.34*	.16	.56***	−.09	−.11	.40**
26) SL Educ Expend	.49***	.32*	.09	.40**	.05	−.17	.26*
27) SL High Expend	.03	−.37**	−.35*	.45**	−.45**	−.23	.33**
28) SL PW Expend	−.02	.16	.12	−.19	.20	.05	.06

TABLE 5–2 (Continued)

	SIMPLE CORRELATION			PARTIAL CORRELATION			R^2
	income/ capita	*urban*	*total income*	*income/ capita*	*urban*	*total income*	
SL Taxes	−.23	−.12	−.06	−.20	.04	.02	.06
St Taxes	−.54***	−.35*	−.30*	−.44**	.08	−.11	.30**
Prop Tax	.55***	.38**	.29*	.43**	−.03	.07	.31**
Sales Tax	−.01	.16	.18	−.18	.16	.13	.07
Excise Tax	.35*	.19	−.06	.33*	.04	−.25	.18*
MV Tax	.22	−.11	−.18	.43**	−.28	−.19	.21*
Income Tax	.25	.05	.13	.29*	−.20	.10	.10
Cur Charges	.33*	.05	−.04	.42**	−.19	−.13	.18*
Debt	.64***	.38**	.44**	.37*	.26	.11	.48***
Rev To St	−.49***	−.62***	−.64***	−.08	−.28	−.45**	.51***
Rev From Non-Loc	−.54***	−.23	−.49***	−.30*	−.09	−.27	.38***
Fed/St	−.46***	−.54***	−.51***	.04	−.17	−.37	.29*
Fed/SL	−.59***	−.60***	−.53***	−.29*	.20	−.28	.46***
Sch Lunch	−.77***	−.65***	−.41**	−.58***	−.23	−.02	.62***
Voc Ed	−.56***	−.43**	−.22	−.41**	−.10	.07	.32**
Rehab Proc	−.35*	−.34*	−.25	−.17	−.10	−.06	.14
Rehab Complet	−.44**	−.40**	−.26	−.24	−.12	−.02	.21*
Sch Compl	.59***	.38**	.31*	.44**	.03	.05	.35***
Exam Success	.52***	.33*	.02	.49***	−.01	−.25	.33***
Total Roads	−.25	−.58***	−.47***	.27	−.49***	−.23	.41***
Rural Roads	.13	−.16	−.31*	.36*	−.20	.31*	.21*
Urban Roads	−.44**	−.67***	−.53***	.07	−.48***	−.24	.48***
Open I System	.03	−.19	.02	.22	−.30*	.10	.09
Paved Roads	.46***	.38**	.31*	.34*	−.06	.14	.23*
Road Safety	.46***	.59***	.42**	.08	.35*	.11	.36***
AFDC Payment	.65***	.48***	.32*	.50***	.03	.03	.43***
OAA Payment	.66***	.45**	.28*	.36*	.11	.00	.31**
AB Payment	.55***	.56***	.29*	.46**	.20	−.08	.46***
APTD Payment	.29*	.33*	.37**	.08	.08	.23	.17
AFDC Recip	.60***	.65***	.38**	.28	.37**	.00	.46***
OAA Recip	.22	.01	−.32*	.36*	−.01	−.44**	.27*

TABLE 5–2 (Continued)

	SIMPLE CORRELATION			PARTIAL CORRELATION			R^2
	income/ capita	urban	total income	income/ capita	urban	total income	
50) AB Recip	.22	.21	.34*	.09	−.04	.27	.12
51) APTD Recip	.11	.32*	.07	−.15	.36*	−.14	.14

† Controlling for each of the other economic variables.
‡ The complete title of each variable is shown in Chapter 2, pp. 34–41.
* Significant at the .05 level.
** Significant at the .01 level.
*** Significant at the .001 level.

well-being and exposure to an urban environment, citizens have greater information about and interest in public affairs; perhaps, too, those who have wealth and control over public policy feel they have less to lose from widespread participation in public affairs. And with high levels of involvement in politics there may be greater electoral incentives for competing elites to develop and solicit popular support. Elsewhere, where politics is relatively closed to public participation, the opportunities for intense inter-party competition are less prominent.

High scores on economic characteristics coexist both with high levels of voter turnout and party competition, and with most measures of state and local government expenditures and public services. It may be a combination of wealth with political participation and competition that affects the nature of government policies. A more active citizenry may express its demands for high quantities and quality of public services. And where parties compete with each other for popular support they might seek support by outbidding one another in the extent of services to be provided.[3]

There are significant exceptions to the stimulative effect of

[3] Ira Sharkansky and Richard I. Hofferbert, "Dimensions of State Politics and Public Services," *American Political Science Review*, LXIII (September 1969).

economic conditions upon government expenditures, public services, and the "progressive" nature of state politics. Economic measures show weak positive relationships, or sizable negative ones, with several measures of educational and highway service, equity in the apportionment of state legislators, the centralization of state-local financial relations, tax effort, and federal aid.

The sizable negative linkages between economic development and the receipt of federal aid reflect the allocation formulae built into many of the grant programs; they redistribute economic resources from wealthy to poorer states. In education it is the programs that are largely supported by the federal government that show inverse relationships with economic resources. The substance of these programs for inexpensive school lunches, vocational education, and vocational rehabilitation seems particularly suited to populations that score low on measures of economic welfare and the magnitude of resources. The negative relationships between economics and the highway programs may likewise reveal this federal effect, or they may reveal the highway-orientations of public officials in underdeveloped rural states.[4]

The negative relationships between economics and the centralization of state-local finances may reflect the differential access of state and local governments to economic resources, and the economic limitations of the tax base that is legally available to local authorities. In a poor state, the access of state authorities to the entire state's economic resources makes them tend to assume a high percentage of state-local financial obligations. State constitutions typically restrict local governments to the tax on real property, and (as demonstrated in Table 5–2) this tax more than others shows a substantial direct association with the level of economic activity. In poor states there are numerous local governments (especially rural counties) that are hard pressed to support a satisfactory level of services on the economic base that lies within their jurisdiction. Perhaps because some localities must rely on state aid in such states, local governments may be generally inclined to rely on the

4 See note 1 above.

revenues of state-collected income and sales taxes in order to minimize the problems associated with high local property taxes. The depression was particularly hard on the property tax; many local governments found it impossible to collect large sums owed them by property owners.[5] And since the depression the real property tax has remained small in the revenue systems of relatively poor states. Public services in poor states, therefore, seem to rely on state financing because local officials face legal restrictions against their use of anything but a property tax and economic problems in raising substantial revenues from such a tax.

The lack of significant positive economic relationships with expenditures of state governments may reflect the fact that state governments are less dependent than local governments on economic conditions. As noted above, state authorities benefit from access to a more extensive and varied economy than local officials and from their legal opportunities to choose among a greater variety of revenue sources. In several instances the governments of poor states spend considerably above the national average because they are responsible for supporting programs that would elsewhere be financed by local governments. Louisiana and Vermont are prominent among the states that have low personal income per capita, but high state government expenditures.[6]

[5] Collections of property taxes by state and local governments declined from $39.74 to $31.93 per capita during the 1927–1936 period, and from 64 to 55 percent of state and local government revenue. See also Dick Netzer, *Economics of the Property Tax* (Washington: The Brookings Institution, 1965).

[6] The scores of these states (along with national averages) on per capita personal income, total state government expenditures per capita, and the percentage of state and local revenue allocated to state agencies provide a vivid illustration of the practice in poor states of allocating a high proportion of financial responsibilities to the state government, and the state government's tendency to make higher expenditures than might be predicted on the basis of wealth alone.

	LOUISIANA	VERMONT	U.S.
income/capita	$1705	$2005	$2212
state and local revenue to state	53.4%	61.8%	41.6%
state expend/capita	$251.74	$255.10	$181.40

Much of the economic-policy relationship described above depends on interstate differences in per capita personal income. This finding is evident in the coefficients of partial correlation shown in Table 5–2, which suggest that personal welfare is a more critical influence upon government decision makers than the incidence of urbanization or the sheer aggregate of economic resources. This finding may reflect the political components in the dependent variables, whereby the individual needs and resources of taxpayers (rather than the total resources or the extent of urbanism within a jurisdiction) are the most salient considerations. Certain exceptions occur in the case of highway expenditures and services. Here there are strong independent relationships with measures of urbanization: the dispersion of population characteristic of a rural state may present physical demands for extensive road networks (relative to population size) that are overwhelming in the perceptions of policy makers.

By themselves, the three economic characteristics leave unexplained much of the interstate variation in public policies. This is evident from the generally low coefficients of multiple determination (R^2) reported in Table 5–2. For only four of the 61 dependent variables do the aggregate of economic measures account for at least half of the interstate variation; these are average salaries of administrators and legislators, the percentage of state and local revenue allocated to the state, and participation in the federal school lunch program. Substantial components of state politics and public policies are not explained by economics alone.

How can we explain the finding that large proportions of interstate variation in political traits are not subject to an economic explanation? The level of economic development may define a range of activity that is feasible; yet it is a broad range, within which political activity or public policy might vary with a given level of economic development. In 1962, for example, Florida and Montana showed similar levels of per capita personal income, but Montana showed the high levels of government expenditure, voter turnout, and party competition typical of the Mountain region while Florida's low scores on the same variables reflected the custom of the Southeast.[7]

Political elites and public officials in the American states obviously take non-economic factors into account when they plan their political strategies or choose among alternative approaches to public policy. Current regional norms and habits or accommodations established in the past by reference to an older set of regional norms might weigh heavily in their decisions.

The regional norms and consultive patterns of public officials in the United States may be more powerful than are economic affinities in uniting the member states of the American regions. Although regional partners *tend to* resemble one another economically, the 17 regions considered in this book are not homogeneous economically. In the next section of this chapter, we shall weigh the importance of economic and non-economic characteristics for the regional patterns of politics and policy.

Economic and Non-Economic Influences on Regional Patterns of Politics and Policy

Both economic and non-economic characteristics of the regions show important relationships with most of the dependent variables. The data of Table 5–3 show that non-economic features are significantly related to fifty measures of state politics and public policy while controlling for the influence of economic conditions; economic characteristics show significant relationships with 57 measures while controlling for other regional attributes. Although for many of the dependent variables it is not feasible to determine whether economic or non-economic factors exert the most direct influence, it is possible in some cases to compare the level of significance reached by

[7] Their respective scores are:

	FLORIDA	MONTANA
income/capita	$2044	$2207
state and local expend/capita	$284.87	$351.51
governor turnout	27.2%	71.6%

TABLE 5–3. ANALYSIS OF COVARIANCE †

DEPENDENT VARIABLES	RELATIONSHIPS BETWEEN ECONOMIC DEVELOPMENT AND DEPENDENT VARIABLES WHILE CONTROLLING FOR REGION			RELATIONSHIPS BETWEEN REGION AND DEPENDENT VARIABLES WHILE CONTROLLING FOR ECONOMIC DEVELOPMENT		
	Demarcation			*Demarcation*		
	1	*2*	*3*	*1*	*2*	*3*
1) U.S. Rep Turn ‡	.14*	.09	.21**	.53***	.54***	.53***
2) Gov Turn	.11*	.07	.16**	.20*	.18*	.22**
3) Lower House Comp	.12*	.03	.20**	.37***	.34***	.49***
4) Upper House Comp	.15**	.08	.23***	.13	.30***	.24**
5) U.S. Rep Comp	.07	.09	.14*	.24**	.17	.14*
6) Gov Comp	.01	.01	.04	.06	.05	.06
7) Gov Tenure	.01	.02	.04	.28**	.14	.15*
8) Lower House Tenure	.05	.08	.05	.14	.30**	.22**
9) Upper House Tenure	.03	.11*	.01	.10	.27**	.14*
10) Schubert-Press	.05	.10*	.04	.14	.14	.08
11) Dauer-Kelsay	.21**	.18**	.21**	.01	−.09	.06
12) David-Eisenberg	.01	.04	.03	.32***	.29**	.16*
13) Legislators	.07	.13*	.02	.18*	.32**	.34***
14) Bills Intro	.44**	.52***	.48***	.02	.17	.17*
15) Bills Pass	.46***	.52***	.42***	.29**	.31**	.15*
16) Legis Session	.12*	.10*	.14*	.03	.08	−.07
17) Legis Compen	.09	.54***	.30**	.09	.21*	.10
18) Employees Salary	.58***	.49***	.70***	.09	.22*	.37***
19) Employees	.14*	.07	.14*	.41***	.38***	.41***
20) Merit System	.18**	.17**	.19**	−.03	.08	.18*
21) Total St Expend	.35**	.45**	.45**	.06	.25**	.37***
22) St Educ Expend	.20**	.24**	.14*	.24*	.34**	.45***
23) St High Expend	.58***	.62***	.64***	.16*	.26*	.28**
24) St PW Expend	.26**	.22**	.22**	.00	.00	−.08

Table 5–3 (Continued)

DEPENDENT VARIABLES	RELATIONSHIPS BETWEEN ECONOMIC DEVELOPMENT AND DEPENDENT VARIABLES WHILE CONTROLLING FOR REGION			RELATIONSHIPS BETWEEN REGION AND DEPENDENT VARIABLES WHILE CONTROLLING FOR ECONOMIC DEVELOPMENT		
	Demarcation			*Demarcation*		
	1	2	3	1	2	3
25) Total SL Expend	.50***	.39**	.57***	.36***	.31**	.45***
26) SL Educ Expend	.32**	.20**	.46**	.57***	.43***	.64***
27) SL High Expend	.62***	.60***	.65***	.32**	.19*	.25**
28) SL PW Expend	.26**	.33**	.26**	.00	.00	−.08
29) SL Taxes	.46***	.49**	.51***	.33**	.22*	.28***
30) St Taxes	.32**	.42**	.41**	.08	.22*	.24***
31) Prop Tax	.24**	.44**	.30**	.34**	.28***	.39***
32) Sales Tax	.33**	.22**	.32**	.05	.06	.08
33) Excise Tax	.50***	.47**	.52***	.12	.20*	.23**
34) MV Tax	.44**	.46**	.41**	.44***	.22*	.15*
35) Income Tax	.26**	.22**	.39**	−.09	.02	.00
36) Cur Charges	.52***	.51***	.50***	.49***	.35***	.31***
37) Debt	.68***	.56***	.75***	.11	.13	.23**
38) Rev To St	.66***	.71***	.75***	−.08	.22*	.24**
39) Rev From Non-Loc	.45**	.64***	.56***	.10	.35***	.45***
40) Fed/St	.51***	.46**	.60***	.57***	.44***	.35***
41) Fed/SL	.58***	.60***	.73***	.11	.22*	.28**
42) Sch Lunch	.54***	.44**	.69***	.30**	.21*	.09
43) Voc Ed	.14*	.20**	.37**	.40***	.21*	.29**
44) Rehab Proc	.22**	.17*	.28**	.10	−.03	.09
45) Rehab Complet	.26**	.26**	.30**	.46***	.28**	.45***
46) Sch Compl	.35**	.42**	.52***	.55***	.64***	.59***
47) Exam Success	.22**	.10*	.37**	.81***	.74***	.63***
48) Total Roads	.61***	.69***	.69***	.13	.18*	.20*
49) Rural Roads	.44**	.50***	.48***	.54***	.39***	.38***
50) Urban Roads	.74***	.68***	.73***	.47***	.53***	.29***
51) Open I System	.32**	.26**	.20**	−.05	−.06	.01

TABLE 5-3 (Continued)

DEPENDENT VARIABLES	RELATIONSHIPS BETWEEN ECONOMIC DEVELOPMENT AND DEPENDENT VARIABLES WHILE CONTROLLING FOR REGION			RELATIONSHIPS BETWEEN REGION AND DEPENDENT VARIABLES WHILE CONTROLLING FOR ECONOMIC DEVELOPMENT		
	Demarcation			*Demarcation*		
	1	2	3	1	2	3
52) Paved Roads	.20**	.30**	.32**	.21*	.35***	.22**
53) Road Safety	.52***	.73***	.71***	.56***	.46***	.54***
54) AFDC Payment	.33**	.39**	.46**	.36**	.20*	.33***
55) OAA Payment	.30**	.35**	.39**	.34**	.21*	.24**
56) AB Payment	.49***	.57***	.53***	.13*	.24**	.08
57) APTD Payment	.39**	.41**	.33*	.38***	.21*	.23*
58) AFDC Recip	.61***	.50**	.65***	−.06	.02	.15*
59) OAA Recip	.53***	.54***	.51***	.18*	.17*	.24**
60) AB Recip	.35**	.20**	.37**	−.07	−.07	−.02
61) APTD Recip	.39**	.41**	.28**	−.01	.19*	.17*

† These data result from three separate analyses, each one made with a different regional demarcation of the states.
‡ The complete title of each variable is shown in Chapter 2, pp. 34–41.
* Significant at the .05 level.
** Significant at the .01 level.
*** Significant at the .001 level.

the intra-class correlation coefficients, and use them to select the stronger independent variables.[8]

[8] It is not feasible to make direct comparisons of the correlation coefficients from the right to the left side of Table 5–3. They represent the products of different analytical techniques: those on the right side show the relationship between a nominal variable and interval variables while controlling for other interval variables; and those on the left side show relationships between interval variables while controlling for a nominal variable. In discerning whether variables depend more on region or economic development, we shall use their level of significance as a measure of relative strength of the coefficients. As in other places throughout this book, the test for significance is not used in the conventional

Non-economic factors of regions are the more salient of the independent variables with respect to measures of voter turnout, party competition, property taxation, the size of state legislatures, spending and service levels in the field of education, and one measure of welfare service (payments for the families of dependent children). Economic conditions seem to be the most salient variables with respect to the state merit system, spending for highways and public welfare, the use of sales, excise, and income taxes, government borrowing, the centralization of state and local government financing, the proportion of state and local revenue received as federal aid, the use of the federal school lunch program, and several measures of highway and welfare service.

Several underlying traits characterize the variables that depend most upon non-economic conditions—and those depending most upon economic ones—within the regions. The variables that are most dependent upon non-economic factors are measures of political practices and institutional forms, plus support for a service (education) that was receiving relatively little federal aid in 1962, when our measurements were made. If there is one trait that each of these variables have in common, it is their isolation from nationwide stimuli directed at their change. The turnout and competition dimensions of state politics appear to be deeply rooted in regional conventions about the proper relationship of citizens to government, or the historic legitimacy of the two major parties. The regional findings for voter turnout might lessen in time with federal intervention in the electoral processes and the maturation of political organizations among nonwhites; and the regional findings for inter-party competition might diminish with the increased legitimacy of the Republican party in the South and that of the Democratic party in northern New England and the Plains regions. Yet the new political forces in the South must fight the apathy of nonvoters among both Negroes and whites as well as the displeasure of rural white

fashion. Because the units of analysis represent a universe (the 48 contiguous states) rather than a sample chosen to represent a larger population, the tests for significance are used to indicate relationships that are "sizable," rather than "significant." For the significance tests employed with the data of Table 5–4 see Blalock, *op. cit.*, Chapter 20.

elites. Although there is significant party competition at the presidential level in almost all states, party competition in state and congressional races must go a long way before both parties have an equal opportunity to attract support in all regions.

If economic development alone were the key to turnout and competition, then the states with the best-developed economies in the South would have shown more political progress than they had by 1962. Texas and Florida led the region (and many non-Southern states) on the three measures of economic development considered in this book, but their levels of voter turnout and party competition still ranked well below the national averages.[9] More than economics, such regional experiences as slavery, the Civil War, the Reconstruction, and continuing racial stereotypes have left their mark on the South.[10]

The regional dependence of spending and service levels in the field of education may reflect a lack of federal involvement in educational service levels and the related "close-to-the-hearth" character of educational policy making. In 1962 state and local activity in the field of education was less dependent on federal grants than were the other major fields of highways and public welfare. Federal funds provided only 5.3 percent of state and local education budgets, but 26.5 percent of highway budgets and 27.8 percent of public welfare. Without federal aid at the level of other services, administrators in the education field also did not have the stimuli of federal standards,

[9] Representative scores indicate that Florida and Texas show lower turnout and competition than the Confederacy, although they score higher on economic development than does the region as a whole.

	FLORIDA	TEXAS	CONFEDERACY	U.S.
governor turnout	27.2%	28.0%	29.4%	52.7%
lower house competition (high scores equal low competition)	94.7	95.3	94.2	70.3
per capita personal income	$2044	$2013	$1716	$2212

[10] Chapter 6 will demonstrate that the Southern regions score markedly lower on measures of voter turnout and party competition than is to be expected on the basis of their economic characteristics alone.

regulations, and recommendations to prod them toward national—as opposed to regional—service norms. Yet the "nonfederal" interpretation of spending and service levels in the field of education runs afoul of the finding that two measures pertaining to federally aided education programs (vocational education and vocational rehabilitation) also show a strong regional dependence, as does one federally aided program in the field of public welfare (payments to families of dependent children). Thus, the close-to-the-hearth character of educational policy making may be the primary factor supporting its regional orientation. This field, as perhaps none other save public safety, is said to lie within the responsibilities and prerogatives of state and local authorities. The "states' rights" effect of education helped to delay the involvement of the federal government with broad-gauged assistance programs, and it may retard the ability of federal standards to break down regional norms.

The public assistance program to provide aid for families of dependent children received much of its funds from the federal government in 1962, but it shows a stronger association with regional norms than economic conditions. It has a long record of being the focus of local (and regional) welfare norms. More than any other program, AFDC bears the brunt of accusations pertaining to welfare cheaters and multigenerational welfarism. While other public assistance programs have shown some relative decline in case loads with the increasing coverage of the Old Age, Survivors, Disability and Health Insurance program, the increasing case loads of AFDC have stood out sharply. As AFDC has consumed an increasing proportion of the public assistance dollar, it has been attacked —especially in the South—with the powerful flails of race and illegitimacy. Opponents have identified AFDC as a Negro program that supports illegitimate children.[11] A former state welfare administrator in the Confederacy told the author that during one recent session of the legislature he had to advertise among the members that forty percent of the AFDC recipients were white.

Two aspects of politics and public policy that have a

11 See Gilbert Y. Steiner, *Social Insecurity: The Politics of Welfare* (Chicago: Rand McNally, 1966), pp. 92–93, 250.

strong regional orientation unaffected by economic conditions may reflect the historical experience and impact of New England. The regional dependence of state legislatures' size reflects the tendency of New England state constitutions to award at least one representative to each town. In 1962 the states of New Hampshire, Vermont, Massachusetts, and Connecticut had 424, 276, 280, and 330 members in their lower houses, respectively, while the national average was 164. The use of the property tax is another historic trait of New England that shows a strong regional dependence. In this case, its heavy use extends not only throughout New England but also into the band of northern states whose initial settlers can be traced back to New England, or intermediate settlements that had themselves been populated with New Englanders. The heavy use of the property tax is found throughout the northeast, and in the Great Lakes, Upper Middle West, and Plains (see Table 3–1).

An underlying characteristic of the variables that depend on economic conditions is their involvement with intergovernmental relations. They include most measures of government spending and public service levels in the fields that benefit from large federal grants (highways and welfare), the proportion of state and local revenues coming from the federal government, and the percentage of state and local revenues allocated to state agencies. These findings point to the economic role of intergovernmental relations. At the federal level, grants-in-aid serve to redistribute economic resources from wealthy states to poor states. The allocation formulae of several grant programs give disproportionate benefits to states that score low on measures of economic capacity (e.g., per capita personal income).[12]

Intergovernmental relations also redistribute wealth at the state level, and these devices are more frequently used in the context of low resources. State revenue systems have access to the entire state and draw resources from wealthy urban areas to support at least minimal service levels in poor counties. State governments have better revenue machinery, as well as a

[12] Advisory Commission on Intergovernmental Relations, *The Role of Equalization in Federal Grants* (Washington: Government Printing Office, 1964), pp. 34 ff.

broader resource base, than local governments. The sales and income taxes employed by state governments seem to work better under adverse economic conditions than the property tax of local governments.[13]

Although it is helpful to identify the variables that depend mostly on economic or non-economic stimuli in the regions, it is necessary to realize that almost all of the dependent variables show significant relationships with *both* categories of influences. In part this reflects the overlapping nature of each region's economic and non-economic experiences. Most regional partners are also economic cousins, and where individual states show a set of political characteristics that are consistent with both their economic and non-economic natures it is both theoretically and practically difficult to identify the root causes. A state's level of economic development is partly a function of regional location. Such regionally conditioned elements as raw materials, natural arteries of transportation, the education and skills of the working force, and popular attitudes about work, investment, and consumption influence present levels of personal well-being, urbanization, and total economic resources—which, in turn, certainly influence the capacity of a region to maintain distinctive patterns in political behavior and public policy. In the South, for example, the forces of wealth and cosmopolitanism associated with increasing levels of personal income and industrialization may be important among the factors that have broken down the region's isolation. Rather than dismissing either economic or non-economic conditions as explanatory variables for regional patterns of state politics and public policy, the findings of this chapter indicate neither potential influence should be considered without reference to the other.

[13] The coefficients of simple (product-moment) correlation between per capita personal income and per capita levels of the property tax, individual income tax, and general sales taxes collected by state and local governments testify to the relative dependence of the property tax on economic resources:

property tax	.55
individual income tax	.25
general sales tax	−.01

We can also use the data of our covariance analysis to judge the saliency of regional demarcations 1, 2, and 3. By comparing the coefficients by demarcation on the right-hand side of Table 5–1 we find that demarcations 2 and 3 provide the sharpest statements of regional peculiarities: 44 and 47 of the variables show a significant association with the non-economic regional variable in those demarcations, whereas only 33 of the variables show such relationships in demarcation 1. The boundaries separating the regions of demarcations 2 and 3 permit more of the regional peculiarities to show through. Recall that demarcation 1 divides the nation into three large regions, principally along the Ohio and Mississippi Rivers, and therefore hides the distinctive traits of the Great Lakes and the Mountain regions. Demarcation 3 differs from 2 in having a larger conception of the South (the Confederacy plus the Border states), and in combining the remaining states into the large regions of Northeast, Northcentral, and Transplains. Even though it does some injustice to Border state peculiarities by placing them with the South, this larger conception of the Southern states is still a highly distinctive grouping.

Summary

Although the economic element is important in the explanation of state politics and public policies, it cannot stand as the only explanation. In this chapter we have seen that three important measures of economic characteristics leave unexplained *most* of the interstate variation in 61 dependent variables. To understand public affairs in the American states, then, one must search beyond per capita personal income, the percentage of population living in urban areas, and total personal income. It is possible that other measures for personal well-being, urbanization, or total economic resources will provide more complete statistical explanations for state politics. Perhaps independent variables that measure the incidence of extreme wealth or poverty in each state or the proportion of population living in metropolitan areas would explain more of the variation in our measures of politics and policy. Yet it is

likely that our findings reveal an important real-world phenomenon: economic factors alone leave unexplained much of
state politics and public policies.

The results of three separate analyses of covariance show
that the regions' non-economic attributes are the strongest determinants of voter turnout and party competition, the size of
state legislatures, several policy measures in the field of education, and the payments given to families of dependent children. Economic explanations are prominent for regional scores
on most highway and public welfare policy measures, and several measures pertaining to federal-state-local or state-local financial relations. The common denominator of variables
showing a strong dependence on non-economic factors is their
relative isolation from nationalizing influences. In contrast,
those variables that show a primary dependence on economic
development are involved with intergovernmental relations;
they testify to the redistributive role that is often played by
federal and state taxes and grants.

Although economic or other explanations are more prominent in the case of certain dependent variables, the findings of
this chapter show that *both* economic and non-economic features of the regions are important in the explanation of almost
all the dependent variables. The two explanations are so in-
terwoven as to confound any simple claim that either economic characteristics of the states or non-economic regional
characteristics serve to explain the current nature of politics or
public policy.

While this chapter has established the importance of region as an independent variable in its own right, it has not
gone far in specifying the non-economic traits of various regions that produce certain features in their states' public
affairs. We have focused not on individual regions but on
aggregates of several regions, as arranged by demarcations 1, 2,
and 3. Chapter 6 returns to the analysis of individual regions,
first by identifying those regions that show higher or lower
scores on each variable than their economic characteristics
alone would indicate, then by assessing the features in the
culture and history of these regions that may have produced
their peculiarities.

6

BEHIND "REGION" AS AN
EXPLANATION OF POLITICS
AND PUBLIC POLICIES

The explanation of the economic correlates of state politics and public policies has been relatively simple: high levels of economic development seem likely to promote interest in voting and tolerance for widespread political participation, competition between parties for electoral support, and generous allotments for government expenditures and public services. Measures of intergovernmental relationship have a special dependence upon economic activity. Where resources are tight there is a tendency to rely more than usual upon the redistributive revenue systems of state and federal authorities.

Pinning down non-economic influences on regional traits, however, is a more elusive task. Region is a diffuse aggregate of economic, social, and political phenomena that include cultural predispositions to particular forms of public service or political relationships; migrations that have transferred practices from one section of the country to another; war and military occupation that have helped to mold nascent prejudices into firm principles of behavior; and the tendency of public officials to select their own norms from those of nearby states. The character and relative importance of these ingredients of "regionalism" vary from one region to another. Moreover, the saliency of specific boundaries between adjacent regions varies with the aspect of state politics or policy that is under consideration: while it is important to distinguish the Mountain region from the Far West when discussing measures of voter turnout, for example, the entire Transmississippi region is a unified whole when the subject is the level of investment in highway programs.

A precise understanding of regional patterns in state politics and public policies demands that we define the peculiarities of each region that do not lend themselves to an explanation in terms of current economic conditions, and then search the culture and history of that region for the phemonena that illuminate each peculiarity. Although we reported regional scores on each dependent variable in Chapter 3, our purpose was merely to identify the character of each regional grouping in relation to others. It was premature to begin the explanation of regional characteristics at that point; any effort to understand the political traits of regions would have floundered on an imperfect understanding of economic traits.

Now we are ready to go behind the regional explanation of state politics and see what it is all about. In this chapter we shall identify those regional traits that persist after considering the economic explanation, and we shall suggest some cultural and historical factors that might account for them.

Techniques

In order to identify those instances where political traits within a region do not respond to economic forces in the usual manner, it is first necessary to define the mathematical relationship that "customarily" prevails between the three measures of economic development and each of the dependent variables. This relationship is expressed in the general form of the regression equation:

$$Y = a + b_1X_1 + b_2X_2 + b_3X_3$$

where Y equals a dependent variable (a measure of state politics or policy); X_1, X_2, and X_3 are the independent variables (per capita personal income, urbanization, and total personal income); and the bs and the a are constants that, when multiplied to the average state score on each independent variable and then summed, approximate the average state score on the dependent variable.[1] By calculating regression equations for each of the 61 dependent variables and then substituting for X_1, X_2, and X_3 the values associated with the average economic characteristics of states in a region, the equations serve to estimate the average score of the region's states on each dependent variable. Then the ratio between the *actual* value and the *estimated* value of a region's score on a dependent variable indicates the extent to which its actual score is above or below the level that is expected on the basis of the economy. Where this ratio is far removed from 1.00 (obtained where the economic characteristics of a region stand in the typical relationship with a dependent variable), it is evident that unusual non-economic factors are at work on a regional characteristic. Thus, the application of a 48-state regression model to each region can identify those regions in which each component of state politics or public policy does not show its "typical" dependence on economic traits. In this chapter we shall concentrate on those cases where a region's actual score on a dependent variable is at least 15 percent above or below the score that is estimated on the basis of its economic characteristics.

The principal task of this chapter is the identification of political characteristics that require explanation by reference to the non-economic characteristics of each region. Thus we shall weed out those "regional traits" that can be explained by reference to economics. Our explanatory efforts will be speculative and drawn primarily from the literature that examines

[1] The regression formulae are specific for each of the 61 dependent variables, and so each formula has individual a and bs computed according to the distribution of the dependent variable. Each formula is computed on the basis of a 48-state sample, and so provides a mathematical statement of the relationship between independent variables and a dependent variable that prevails nationwide.

state politics within several regions. They are reported to provide examples of the diverse and complex non-economic factors that might influence regional characteristics. Thorough investigations of culture and history, and of the behavior of state elites, will produce a better understanding of the origin and perpetuation of regional traits than can be presented in this book.

Non-Economic Explanations for Regional Traits

NEW ENGLAND

Several distinctive traits of the New England region reflect peculiarities of its culture and history. As shown in Table 6–1, New England state legislatures are larger, more active, better apportioned, but not as well-paid as might be expected on the basis of economic conditions; spending for education and the use of vocational education is lower than expected; road systems are less developed and there is less use of the major state taxes (retail sales and individual income) than is expected. The critical phenomena in the New England background may include an ambivalence toward local autonomy that couples a long tradition of locally oriented political mechanisms with a lack of "home rule"; an upper-class "Yankee" private school tradition and an extensive system of Roman Catholic parochial schools; well-organized political parties (especially in the southernmost states of Massachusetts, Rhode Island, and Connecticut) and an urban orientation that extends far back into the region's history.

The large size of the New England state legislatures reveals the prominence of the town as a unit of government and the custom of providing each town with at least one state legislator. While the 48-state average number of state legislators is 164, the New England states of New Hampshire and Vermont have 424 and 276 legislators, respectively; Connecticut has 330 and Massachusetts 280. In some towns of rural New England the residents have virtually drafted delegates to the state capitol; members of these communities have consented to serve one term on each occasion that the chore is passed to them.

The low pay of legislators signifies the amateurish character of the assignment. Although Massachusetts pays a professional rate of $16,800 for the biennium, all other states in the region pay well below the $7,106 national average. Rhode Island and New Hampshire are the most stingy; they pay $600 and $200 to their legislators every two years. Another reflection of New England localism is the relatively low reliance on taxes that provide the bulk of state-collected revenues in other regions. Relative to its economic position, New England scores low in its reliance on the individual income tax and lowest of all the regions in its use of the general sales tax. On the property tax—the historic bulwark of local revenue systems—New England scores above the level that is associated with its economic development. Although a recent (1966) sales tax enactment by Massachusetts may help align the region's revenue systems to those of other sections, the long struggle preceding the Massachusetts sales tax indicated severe resistance to the innovation. As late as 1962, Massachusetts' state and local governments received 53 percent of their tax revenue from the property tax, while governments throughout the country drew only 30 percent of their revenue from this source.[2]

The size of New England state legislatures, the amateurish level of their members' salaries, and the states' failure to exploit state-collected taxes reveal a localistic background that had its origin in Colonial times. The first settlers in the northern colonies were Congregationalists whose concern for local autonomy extended to politics as well as religion. However, the large volume of state legislative business in New England highlights an ambivalence toward local autonomy. Much of the business transacted in New England legislatures deals with the minutiae of local bills. State legislators must decide about the location of school building , mass transit routes, and other public facilities.

The high scores of the New England region on the measures of equitable legislative apportionment reflect both the localism of the area and the strength of political parties. Par-

[2] See my "Economic and Political Correlates of State Government Expenditures: General Tendencies and Deviant Cases," *Midwest Journal of Political Science*, XI (May 1967), 173–192.

TABLE 6–1. RATIOS BETWEEN ACTUAL REGIONAL SCORES AND THOSE SCORES

RATIOS	NORTH	NO-EAST	NEW ENG	MID ATL	GRT LAKES	PLAINS	NO-CENTRAL
1) U.S. Rep Turn ‡	1.041	1.078	1.106	.893	1.129	1.081	1.101
2) Gov Turn	.961	.953	.997	.837*	1.057	1.022	1.037
3) Lower House Comp	.838*	.847*	.891	.892	.723*	.805*	.772*
4) Upper House Comp	1.089	1.096	1.104	1.189*	.986	1.002	.996
5) U.S. Rep Comp	.973	.984	.991	1.005	.922	.958	.944
6) Gov Comp	.975	.961	.945	1.027	.963	.936	.947
7) Gov Tenure	.976	1.012	.983	1.062	.890	.911	.902
8) Lower House Tenure	1.026	1.045	1.071	1.058	.937	.963	.952
9) Upper House Tenure	1.037	1.009	.946	1.053	1.028	.933	.972
10) Schubert-Press	1.212*	1.280*	1.260*	1.108	1.263*	.743*	.959
11) Dauer-Kelsay	1.031	1.068	1.070	.932	1.082	1.032	1.053
12) David-Eisenberg	1.194*	1.246*	1.352*	1.038	1.186*	.866	1.007
13) Legislators	1.227*	1.472*	1.757*	.909	.967	.936	.950
14) Bills Intro	1.094	1.487*	1.997*	1.214*	.500*	.894	.639*
15) Bills Pass	.976	1.089	1.441*	.927	.685*	.809*	.743*
16) Legis Session	1.101	.957	1.177*	.798*	1.337*	1.088	1.206*
17) Legis Compen	1.147	1.016	.769*	1.198*	1.312*	1.170*	1.258*
18) Employees Salary	.985	.975	.988	.940	1.029	.987	1.006
19) Employees	.939	.935	.926	.945	.950	1.027	.995
21) Total St Expend	.930	.928	.941	.956	.889	.876	.881
22) St Educ Expend	.719*	.608*	.583*	.855	.741*	.762*	.753*
23) St High Expend	.931	.972	1.109	.747*	.976	.938	.923
24) St PW Expend	.897	.954	1.053	.778*	.822*	1.011	.929
25) Total SL Expend	.921	.939	.960	.874	.927	.985	.960
26) SL Educ Expend	.886	.837*	.847*	.854	.964	1.019	.995
27) SL High Expend	.830*	.893	.994	.657*	.809*	.957	.900
28) SL PW Expend	.898	.965	1.064	.755*	.854	1.053	.962
29) SL Taxes	.999	1.031	1.049	.952	.984	1.032	1.012
30) St Taxes	.929	.894	.893	1.036	.875	.807*	.834*

‡ The complete title of each variable is shown in Chapter 2, pp. 34–41.
* Ratios removed from 1.00 by at least 15 percent.

ESTIMATED FOR EACH REGION ON THE BASIS OF ECONOMIC CHARACTERISTICS

PP MID- WEST	BORDER	SO- EAST	SOUTH	CONFED	SO- WEST	MOUNTNS	FAR WEST	TRANS- PLAINS	TRANS- MISS
157*	.923	.713*	.742*	.623*	1.021	1.298*	.904	1.105	1.082
024	1.041	.789*	.793*	.666*	.905	1.213*	.874	1.036	1.013
694*	.910	1.006	1.018	1.052	.920	.729*	.806*	.744*	.811*
015	1.007	1.116	1.149	1.188*	1.168*	.814*	1.190*	.993	1.022
888	.966	1.078	1.069	1.112	.948	.891	1.141	.971	.971
895	.959	1.097	1.071	1.124	.902	.949	1.078	.983	.958
883	1.028	1.126	1.102	1.155*	.854	.990	1.032	.950	.940
959	1.093	1.043	1.059	1.046	1.074	.781*	.971	.902	.941
015	1.104	1.044	1.066	1.050	1.105	.844*	.863	.901	.932
727*	.758*	.887	.839*	.897	.666*	1.219*	.971	1.045	.893
110	.967	.955	.939	.937	.977	1.005	.992	.983	1.007
078	.967	.942	.905	.880	.655*	.967	.901	.899	.859
986	1.108	.942	1.004	.969	1.129	.667*	.630*	.653*	.851
987	.890	1.327*	1.148	1.189*	.675*	.696*	.644*	.682*	.721*
784*	.777*	1.397*	1.276*	1.430*	.595*	.610*	1.062	.827*	.791*
489*	1.117	.893	.958	.938	1.147	.663*	.959	.865	.973
772*	1.161*	.881	.946	.890	.844*	.637*	.735*	.710*	.866
101	.949	.973	.958	.957	1.019	1.041	1.084	1.071	1.028
001	.931	.964	.964	.976	1.027	1.138	1.106	1.111	1.071
027	1.022	.972	.988	.944	1.152*	1.659*	1.287*	1.211	1.075
980	.971	.924	.952	.911	1.171*	1.128	1.279*	1.243*	1.044
913	.902	.864	.878	.849*	1.168*	1.473*	1.081	1.295*	1.135
896	1.355*	.977	1.025	.898	1.152*	.978	1.336	1.072	1.096
072	.888	.915	.907	.908	1.050	1.162*	1.131	1.147	1.073
102	.883	.860	.875	.858	1.111	1.217*	1.136	1.199*	1.111
946	.725*	.761*	.762*	.778*	1.006	1.227*	.902	1.072	1.019
036	1.192*	.917	.944	.846*	1.059	1.022	1.141	1.024	1.065
097	.916	.938	.936	.939	1.028	1.110	1.062	1.087	1.057
975	1.086	1.034	1.053	1.014	1.087	.978	1.239*	1.096	.987

TABLE 6–1 (Continued)

RATIOS	NORTH	NO-EAST	NEW ENG	MID ATL	GRT LAKES	PLAINS	NO-CENTR.
31) Prop Tax	.974	1.055	1.116	.769*	1.041	1.150*	1.10
32) Sales Tax	.817*	.631*	.623*	.644*	1.181*	.860	1.01
33) Excise Tax	.990	1.076	1.082	1.012	.849*	.832*	.83
34) MV Tax	.926	.924	.872	.852	1.084	1.106	1.09
35) Income Tax	1.033	.934	.766*	1.711*	.505*	.784*	.66
36) Cur Charges	.848*	.786*	.694*	.941	.939	1.021	.98
37) Debt	1.034	1.069	1.039	1.218*	.818*	.834*	.82
38) Rev To St	1.018	1.093	1.092	1.075	.858	.888	.87
39) Rev From Non-Loc	1.030	1.071	1.082	.921	1.089	1.216*	1.15
41) Fed/SL	.902	.972	1.004	.825*	.826*	.890	.86
42) Sch Lunch	.913	.875	.861	1.019	.894	1.087	1.01
43) Voc Ed	.729*	.594*	.628*	.733*	.849*	.967	.92
44) Rehab Proc	.978	1.070	1.061	1.175*	.712*	.924	.75
45) Rehab Complet	1.178*	1.186*	1.034	1.930*	.810*	.754*	.77
46) Sch Compl	.987	.951	.931	.948	1.092	1.146	1.12
47) Exam Success	.933	.941	.977	.837*	.983	1.101	1.05
48) Total Roads	.696*	.788*	.726*	.872*	.479*	.770*	.69
49) Rural Roads	.417*	.386*	.300*	.346*	.741*	1.224*	1.08
50) Urban Roads	.720*	.702*	.777*	.522*	.821*	1.322*	1.14
51) Open I System	1.047	1.069	1.121	.889	1.139	1.037	1.08
52) Paved Roads	1.068	1.061	1.117	.951	1.134	1.068	1.09
53) Road Safety	1.179*	1.335*	1.435*	1.134	.953	.978	.96
54) AFDC Payment	1.020	1.068	1.089	.912	1.063	1.106	1.08
55) OAA Payment	.979	1.002	1.014	.889	1.036	1.478*	1.09
56) AB Payment	.979	1.043	1.118	.822*	.986	1.101	1.05
57) APTD Payment	1.111	1.125	1.232*	.938	1.165*	1.124	1.14
58) AFDC Recip	.970	1.039	.975	1.102	.809*	.691*	.75
59) OAA Recip	.436*	.569*	.563*	.310*	.248*	.485*	.42
60) AB Recip	1.257*	1.380*	.885	1.909*	1.001	.882	.93
61) APTD Recip	.852	.058*	.953	.890	.688*	.662*	.67

PP MD- EST	BORDER	SO- EAST	SOUTH	CONFED	SO- WEST	MOUNTNS	FAR WEST	TRANS- PLAINS	TRANS- MISS
156*	.583*	.686*	.665*	.733*	.814*	1.138	.825*	.960	1.012
809*	1.108	1.168*	1.031	.998	.997	.883	1.817	1.335*	1.092
838*	.970	1.089	1.078	1.113	.867	.866	1.127	.915	.910
105	.855	.716*	.821*	.822*	1.486*	1.288*	1.201*	1.231*	1.227*
180*	1.759*	.970	1.272*	.849*	1.056	1.522*	.823*	1.173*	.984
086	.905	.990	1.003	1.037	1.217*	1.115	1.217*	1.170*	1.121
874	1.182*	1.176*	1.203*	1.143	.994	.813*	1.089	.946	.924
838*	1.103	1.016	1.040	1.008	1.136	.993	1.100	1.044	1.000
092	.829*	.919	.883	.936	.854	1.021	.856	.916	1.017
762*	.980	.956	.951	.953	1.084	1.232*	1.255*	1.212*	1.078
042	1.059	1.074	1.056	1.068	.879	.988	.959	.964	.997
127	.896	1.111	1.141	1.221*	1.005	1.035	1.641*	1.121	1.092
936	1.450*	1.145	1.168*	.995	.798*	.957	.709*	.765*	.819*
821*	1.613*	1.366*	1.385*	1.266*	.739	.938	.838*	.820*	.133*
186*	.923	.891	.900	.898	.983	1.076	1.011	1.039	1.069
061	.907	.813*	.837*	.808*	1.043	1.153*	.961	1.059	1.072
621*	1.052	1.063	1.050	1.067	1.696*	1.435*	1.327*	1.452*	1.145
110	.445*	.588*	.592*	.768*	2.126*	1.994*	1.613*	1.849*	1.610*
209*	.737*	.818*	.840*	.903	1.186*	1.067	.851	.991	1.152*
167*	.964	.778*	.834*	.793*	1.273*	.809*	1.005	.966	1.021
102	.957	.951	.937	.934	.784*	.961	.974	.925	.968
029	1.029	1.041	1.005	.980	.685*	.748*	.703*	.697*	.796*
235*	.882	.810*	.812*	.751*	1.042	1.175*	.932	1.068	1.069
220*	.861	.877	.886	.894	1.030	1.054	1.045	1.035	1.079
147	.891	.910	.910	.909	1.105	1.002	1.090	1.043	1.075
295*	.983	.822*	.863	.795*	1.071	.998	.765*	.922	1.003
775*	1.213*	1.085	.998	.796*	1.033	1.114	1.191*	1.205*	.992
492*	.425*	1.197*	.818*	1.612*	1.828*	1.762*	2.160*	1.907*	1.373*
657*	1.344*	1.234*	1.248*	1.274*	1.392*	.792*	1.828*	1.322*	1.158*
624*	.949	.991	.912	.888	.673*	1.589*	1.757*	1.460*	1.130

ticularly in the southern tier of New England, where the parties have been intensely competitive since the 1930's, the major parties are also well organized in the state legislatures.[3] Thus, local political leaders can employ the mechanisms of integrated political parties in order to maintain their communities' share of representation.[4] Although the gerrymander drew its name from the contorted districts of Massachusetts, that state scores considerably above the national average on all three measures of apportionment equity.[5]

New England's private school emphasis—a combination of elite Yankee schools and Roman Catholic parochial schools —works against the region's expenditures for education and their use of one federal program (for vocational education) that is not generally available to private school pupils. Now the incidence of Roman Catholic parochial education far outweighs the older tradition represented by Groton, Andover, Exeter, and Saint Mark's. In the heavily Catholic states of Rhode Island and Massachusetts, 29.4 and 23.6 percent of the elementary and secondary school pupils attend non-public institutions. In the field of higher education, the status and facilities of Harvard, Massachusetts Institute of Technology, Yale, Brown, and Dartmouth have long been above the major public institutions in their states. As late as 1964, tiny Amherst College (1,100 students) reported more volumes in its library than the University of Massachusetts (8,500 students). On the important variables that measure the success of state school systems by means of school completions and exam success, the New England region scores only slightly below the

[3] Duane Lockard, *New England State Politics* (Princeton: Princeton University Press, 1959), pp. 151, 203, 244, 324.

[4] Thomas R. Dye suggested this interpretation of the link between party organization and apportionment equity.

[5] The Massachusetts and U.S. average scores on the three measures of apportionment equity are:

	MASSACHUSETTS	U.S.
Schubert-Press	80.4	47.7
Dauer-Kelsay	91.0	67.1
David-Eisenberg	102.0	63.6

level associated with its economic development. Therefore, the mixture of private and public education and resulting low levels of government expenditure for education do not impede educational programs. But the private school emphasis does figure in the politics of New England education: supporters of parochial schools argue that public authorities have an obligation to provide financial support for the thousands of students in private schools, while spokesmen for public education feel that their own efforts are subverted by private school parents who oppose increased school taxes.

In scoring lower than expected on both rural and municipal road mileage, the New England region typifies the relatively low emphasis on highway services that is found in all of the older and congested sections of the United States. Part of the explanation may lie in the "efficiency" of roads in congested sections; each mile of road carries more traffic than a mile of rural highway in the uncongested West. Some commentators have perceived a combination of deterring costs and low concern as the explanation for "underdeveloped" road networks in such regions as New England, Middle Atlantic, and Great Lakes. Each mile of new road that is built in the congested sections of these regions is likely to upset existing landowners, and with relatively short distances between population centers drivers may have become used to the problems of heavy traffic.[6] New England's high score on the road safety measure suggests that people have coped with congestion by doing relatively little driving.

MIDDLE ATLANTIC

The distinctive traits of the Middle Atlantic region include lower scores on voter turnout than expected on the basis of its economic development, relatively low spending and service levels in the highway field, low scores on a measure of educational service (exam success), low reliance on property and sales taxation, and high reliance on income taxation and government borrowing. The regional traits that help to explain these oddities include high rates of immigration and

6 Thomas R. Dye, *Politics, Economics and the Public: Policy Outcomes in the American States* (Chicago: Rand McNally, 1966), p. 161.

population mobility within the New York-Washington mega-lopolis, and long-standing tax traditions.

The relatively low scores on both voter turnout and exam success may reflect the continuing influx of migrants to the large cities of New York, New Jersey, Pennsylvania, and Maryland, and a resulting high level of cultural dissonance. Although measures of economic development show close positive relationships with measures of turnout and educational success (see Table 5–2), the enormous wealth of the Middle Atlantic region may deter high scores on these dependent variables. Historically the wealth has attracted poor Europeans and more recently migrants from the rural South and the Carribean; the urban ghettoes reflect both the appealing economic vitality of their cities and an unfortunate distribution of economic rewards. The working-class migrants attracted to Middle Atlantic states have probably depressed the region's scores on voter turnout and exam success, and the middle- and upper-class residents of the urban conglomeration may diminish voter turnout further by virtue of their own mobility. The region scores lower on turnout for state elections than national elections, suggesting that highly mobile residents are most likely to avoid the less familiar terrain of state elections.

The high reliance on government borrowing in the Middle Atlantic region may reflect the tax crises that two states have experienced in recent years. Both New York and New Jersey have enacted statewide general sales taxes, but these enactments reflect a marked break with political tradition and came only after protracted executive-legislative struggles. Because existing tax structures could not produce revenues to meet demands for service, and because members of the executive and legislature could not agree on an easier solution to revenue needs, the road to government borrowing may have looked especially tempting. Traditionally, New York relied upon a relatively progressive individual income tax. As late as 1962, state and local governments in New York received 19 percent of their revenue from such a tax, as against the national average of 7 percent. In the case of New Jersey, the tradition was to avoid broad-based state taxes. Until 1966 the state was one of two holdouts (with Nebraska) against either an income or sales tax. At the state level the major income producer was the gasoline tax. State funds were so sparse in New Jersey during the early 1960's that Rutgers University built new classrooms on the ground floors of student dormitories. The students helped to pay for these classrooms with their room fees.

GREAT LAKES

The distinctive traits of the Great Lakes region include higher scores on party competition and legislative-apportionment equity than normally occur at that level of economic development, and lower scores on income taxation and government indebtedness. The origins of these traits may be found in the recent history of political parties in the region, and in the prohibitions against indebtedness and income taxation to be found in several state constitutions.

Although the Lakes region shows the highest scores relative to economic status on certain measures of party competition, it is not so long ago that the region was a Republican area. Austin Ranney's index of state party competition during the 1946–1963 period, for example, places all the states in the region below .4 on a scale that extended from 0.0 (one-party Republican) to 1.0 (one-party Democratic). Yet by 1962 all the states but Ohio showed party competition in the lower house that was within 6 percent of a 50-50 split. The recent development of party competition in the Lake states may reflect the attraction of its growing industrial cities for Southern migrants (who come with Democratic inclinations) plus the strength added to the Democratic party by developing labor unions and (in Wisconsin) the inheritance of the Progressive party. The strong party organizations may be an important element in the cities' ability to get relatively fair representation in the state legislatures. Where a city's delegation to the legislature can rely on its party leaders to provide some continuity in supporting their members' needs, the delegates may use the party vehicle to obtain a fair share of seats.

For the immediate explanation of the Lakes region's low scores on income taxation and government indebtedness, we need look no further than state constitutions. Those of Michigan and Illinois restrict the taxation of personal incomes, and those of Indiana, Michigan, Ohio, and Wisconsin put severe limitations upon government borrowing. Although the Lake states evade their own constitutional limitations by allowing public corporations to issue "non-guaranteed" bonds (e.g., for college dormitories and toll roads), it is apparent that the very fact of restrictions against borrowing by governments has a limiting effect on total indebtedness.[7] What historical experience of the region lies behind the unusually restrictive limitations on government borrowing? The restrictions appeared in those states' constitutions during the nineteenth century, partly in response to a rash of defaulted bond issues that had been used to support turnpikes, railroads, and canals. In response to their overextended obligations, Midwestern politicians wrote fiscal conservatism into their state constitutions and it became part of the region's norms.

UPPER MIDDLE WEST

The Upper Middle West overlaps the Great Lakes region but shows several distinctive characteristics that might not be expected from its level of economic development. The region, which includes Michigan, Wisconsin, Minnesota, and North Dakota, shows a high reliance on property and personal income taxes, a tendency to give an unusually high proportion of financial responsibilities to local governments, and generous payments to welfare recipients. Behind these traits there stands a history of initial settlement by former New Englanders, and a long-standing reputation for "progressivism."

The New England heritage of the Upper Middle West is

---

[7] It is not the state or the local government, as such, but special corporations that issue the bonds, which are "non-guaranteed" in the sense that the state (or local) government does not guarantee their payment with its full faith and credit. Rather, the corporation established to construct college dormitories or a toll road pledges the income from its about-to-be-constructed facility for the bond's repayment. The non-guaranteed bonds typically require the payment of a higher rate of interest than bonds guaranteed by government agencies, and this higher rate of interest works to keep borrowing below the level normally associated with the level of economic development that prevails through the Lake states. See James A. Maxwell, *Financing State and Local Governments* (Washington: The Brookings Institution, 1965), p. 198.

apparent in the region's heavy reliance on the property tax and its tendency to assign considerable responsibilities to local governments. The early settlers in Wisconsin also implanted a township form of government; town meetings still function in rural areas of that state in much the same way that they operate in New England.

The progressive nature of government in the Upper Middle West has shown itself in the Progressive party of Wisconsin, the alliance of liberal intellectuals with the Auto Workers' Union in the Michigan Democratic party, and the labor-farmer alliances represented by the Farmer-Labor party in Minnesota and the Non-Partisan League in North Dakota. In public services, a similar progressivism is apparent in the well-developed public schools and state universities in Michigan, Wisconsin, and Minnesota, as well as innovative activities in welfare, corrections, and workmen's compensation. In our data these activities show themselves as high scores in school completions, and in the generosity of public assistance payments. In the field of taxation, Wisconsin led the nation with the development of a progressive-rate income tax in 1911, and as late as 1962 both Wisconsin and Minnesota were among the states that relied most heavily on this revenue device.[8]

PLAINS

The Plains states partly overlap the Upper Middle West; the two regions shared an initial settlement pattern that drew heavily from New England and other states that had received an initial New England settlement. This residue appears in a heavier reliance on locally raised property taxes than economic characteristics would lead one to expect, and a disinclination toward state-collected income and sales taxes. Until a 1966 revenue crisis, Nebraska persisted in the heavy use of property taxes which were collected locally and then allocated to the state government. In 1960 the Nebraska state government received about 30 percent of its revenues from the property tax while state governments generally received only 3 percent of their revenue from this source.

[8] During that year Minnesota received 12.9 percent of its revenue from income taxes, and Wisconsin 15.3 percent. The national average was only 6.9 percent.

MOUNTAIN

The Mountain region was the last major settlement area in the continental United States and reveals the lateness of its development in several aspects of state politics and public policy, primarily in competitive party systems. More than any other region, the Mountain states show consistently higher scores on the measures of competition than would be expected on the basis of economic development.[9] This competitiveness originated in the party loyalties brought to the area after the Civil War by Northern and Southern migrants. Since that time no sectional trauma has aligned the residents of Mountain states into one party or the other, and the result is a carryover until today of two viable parties.

It is not only in the level of party competition that the Mountain region shows traits at odds with its economic development. The region is one of the most distinctive in the variety of features that are regionally unique. Its turnout rates are the highest in the nation, and appear even higher in the context of low economic development; its state legislatures are small, inactive, and poorly paid; and despite a certain reputation for conservatism the state and local governments of the Mountain region show among the highest scores on measures of spending, federal aid, and the outputs of public services.

The high scores on voter turnout in the Mountain states may reflect the excitement of competitive party politics, or the absence of large groups of culturally distinct residents who would stay away (or be kept away) from public affairs. The Mountain states have not attracted large numbers of Negroes, perhaps because the economy has been relatively stagnant.

The economic condition of the Mountain region is partly responsible for its high reliance on federal aid. Many federally aided programs purposely redistribute resources from "have" to "have-not" states, and the below-average personal income

9 While the low level of economic development in the Mountains bears some resemblance to the Southern economy, the two regions contrast markedly in the nature of party competition. By themselves, the Mountain and Southern regions demonstrate the weakness in the economic explanation for party competition. See Richard E. Dawson and James A. Robinson, "Interparty Competition, Economic Variables and Welfare Politics in the American States," *Journal of Politics,* XXV (May 1963), 265–289.

in the Mountain states permits them to receive extra alloca-
tions of federal assistance. Moreover, an unusually large
amount of the land area in the Mountain region is held by the
federal government, and western congressmen have won acceptance of the notion that Washington should give additional support to states with large acreage in the public do-
main. More than 30 percent of the land in each Mountain
state is owned by federal agencies.

Mountain state legislatures are generally small, inactive,
and poorly paid, but this is no sign of weak government. On
the measures of government expenditure and public services,
the region does considerably better than expected on the basis
of its economic development. Relative to economic conditions
its expenditures are the highest of any region in the country;
it ranks at or near the top in the measures of total road mileage, the success of residents on a national educational examination, the generosity of welfare payments for families of
dependent children, and the recipient rates for Old Age Assistance and Aid to the Permanently and Totally Disabled.
These traits suggest a community-minded culture that stands in
odd contrast to the success that right-wing Republicans have
recently enjoyed in Montana, Wyoming, and Idaho. Several ingredients of the region's history may explain the "progressive"
nature of public services: the radical labor movements that
developed in the late nineteenth and early twentieth centuries
out of the hardships in mining and lumber camps; the great
distances, severe terrain, and isolation of population that
might have enforced a certain amount of cooperation (at the
same time they provided a rationale for extreme individual-
ism); and the absence of large cultural minorities whose extreme poverty or distinctiveness might discourage the dominant population groups from accepting heavy tax levies. Thus,
the cultural homogeneity, the severity of the environment,
and the reaction to earlier excesses of a free-enterprise economy may have combined to mold the distinctive politics and
public policies.

WESTERN HIGHWAY POLICIES

A combination of traits that appears generally throughout
the western regions (Southwest, Mountain, Far West, Trans-

plains, and Transmississippi) includes highway services and motor vehicle taxes considerably higher than expected on the basis of economic characteristics, and road safety scores that are considerably below expectations. These figures point to a section where automobile and truck transportation is heavily relied on, road users are fair game for the tax collector, and highway carnage is proportionately high. Perhaps the great distance between population centers, requiring relatively high investments in road mileage relative to population, is at the heart of this highway orientation in western politics. In the Mountain states the terrain makes these miles difficult and costly to construct. Because it is acceptable across the country for "users' taxes" to pay for highways,[10] the costs of road investment create high taxes on motor vehicles and drivers. Furthermore, the incidence of auto travel seems to generate high mortality rates.

SOUTH

The major Southern regions (South, Southeast, and Confederacy) show a number of the traits that are claimed for them by political scientists and historians, even after controlling for their low levels of economic development. They score significantly lower than expected on voter turnout and party competition, and in the provision of services in the fields of education, highways, and public welfare.

Because the low turnout and single-party character of Southern politics is not explained by the poverty of the region, we must look to centuries of slavery and segregation, together with the corollaries of elitism, the alien reputation of the Republican party, and the reluctance of white politicians to carry their competition outside of the Democratic party. The effects of this narrow base of Southern politics show themselves in the low levels of public service and the regressive nature of state tax systems. The region scores below economic expectations on the measures of school completion, exam success, urban and rural road mileage, and benefit payments in all of the major public-assistance programs. Its performance in the

10 Philip H. Burch, *Highway Revenue and Expenditure Policy in the United States* (New Brunswick: Rutgers University Press, 1962).

program to aid families of dependent children is particularly poor, and reflects AFDC's reputation for being a "Negroes' program." Similarly, the low regional scores on exam success reflect the cultural distance between Southern Negroes and the dominant American society, and the failure of Southern school systems to close the gap since the Emancipation. The only services in which the South scores high (relative to economic status) are the three educational programs that receive much of their support from the federal government, and which threaten the *least* disruption of the social system: school lunches, vocational education, and vocational rehabilitation.

The regressive nature of Southern revenue systems is apparent in the low reliance on income taxes and the relatively high use of sales and excise taxes.[11] Part of the explanation for the Southern revenue pattern can be found in the area's extreme poverty, which hinders the efficient collection of a tax on personal incomes. The sales tax wins support partly because it is collected in tolerably small portions. Indeed, Mississippi pioneered in the development of the state retail sales tax during the depression when it sold tokens and collected mil taxes on the very smallest sales. Yet there is also a racial ingredient in the South's reliance on the sales tax: several state officials in the Confederacy have praised the levy on retail sales because it "makes the niggers pay their share."

Another trait of the South is hyperactive state legislatures. More than in any other region except New England, Southern legislatures introduce and pass an annual torrent of bills. In the South this reflects a centralization of government at the state level that has existed since colonial times, when the South lacked sufficient population or the inclination to develop numerous small towns. The legislatures' current activity includes the passage of many local bills. Southern legislatures serve policy-making functions that are provided elsewhere by local councils. Another reflection of the centralization found in Southern governments is their low use of the property tax. Throughout the country this tax is the mainstay of local reve-

---

[11] The generally progressive nature of state income taxes and the regressive nature of sales and excise taxes is described in George Bishop, "Tax Burden by Income Class," *National Tax Journal*, XIV (March 1961).

nue systems, but Southern regions make less use of it than is expected from their economic conditions. Much of the money that Southern governments spend comes from sales and excise taxes collected by the states and either spent directly by state agencies or redistributed to counties and municipalities.

BORDER REGIONS

Around the edges of the South, two border regions show certain traits of the South (after controlling for economic characteristics), but on other dimensions they bear greater resemblance to their non-Southern neighbors. The regions at issue are the Border states and the Southwest. Each of them shows the Southern trait of low reliance on the real property tax, and the Border states show low scores on highway services. Yet the Border states resemble other middlewestern states in having higher scores than expected on some measures of welfare services. The Southwest shows the distinctively western traits of high scores on motor vehicle taxation and highway services, and a poor highway safety record.

One trait on which the Southwest stands out is its inequity in legislative apportionment; in this, it is at polar opposites from New England. The regional contrasts may be explained by another dimension (not subject to measurement in this book): the strength of party organizations. In the state legislatures of New England party leaders exercise considerable control over their members, but the two parties in Southwestern legislatures are little more than holding companies whose members tend to vote on the basis of non-party cues.[12] Urban representatives in New England, but not in the Southwest, can use their party institutions to maintain fair representation for their communities.

Summary

This chapter has identified those regional traits in state politics that are *not explained* by reference to the level of

----

12 See, for example, Samuel C. Patterson, "Dimensions of Voting Behavior in a One-Party State Legislature," *Public Opinion Quarterly*, XXVI (Summer 1962), 185–200.

economic development within the regions. There are many such traits, but once the economic explanation has been found wanting, no other single set of phenomena accounts successfully for them. For some findings the political attitudes and values of original settlers or large groups of subsequent migrants may have been critical. Locally oriented administration and the heavy use of local revenue sources is evident in New England and in several other regions (Great Lakes, Upper Middle West, and Plains) that received many settlers either directly from New England or from intermediate regions settled by New Englanders. Similarly, the high level of party competition in the Mountain region seems to have drawn its stimulus from early settlers, both Republican and Democratic, who migrated from both North and South after the Civil War.

When highway services, motor vehicle taxes, and fatality rates are examined on a regional basis, they seem to depend on the diffusion or congestion of population. In the Northeast and Middle West the states tend to show low scores on highway services, low motor vehicle taxes, and enviable safety records. These findings may reflect the efficiency of roads in congested areas, the reluctance of their governments to provoke the antagonisms that accompany major highway projects, plus the minimal use of automobile transportation in congested states. The enviable safety record in the Northeast may represent nothing more than a tendency to do less driving than residents in more scattered parts of the country. Western states, on the other hand, score well on measures of highway mileage relative to population and show a high reliance on motor vehicle taxes (used to pay for road improvements); their residents also kill each other on the highways at a greater rate than elsewhere.

The factors that appear most responsible for the peculiar traits of the South have been well documented in the existing literature: the War and Reconstruction, racial antagonisms left over from slavery and segregation, continuing poverty, and the conservative inclinations of white elites. This chapter has added nothing to the explanation of Southern traits, but it has shown that the South shows markedly low levels of voter turnout, inter-party competition, and levels of public service even after controlling for its low level of economic development.

In some cases, regional traits may first have formed as reactions against earlier political practices. Thus, the debt restrictions in the constitutions of the Great Lake states—initially written to avoid a repetition of excessive government borrowing for public works—remain today as deterrents to government borrowing. And the generous public services and high level of state and local government expenditures in the Mountain region may have begun partly in reaction against the *laissez-faire* excesses of the early lumber and mineral barons. Another reaction may have started in the Mountain region; during recent years conservative Republicans have won important offices in Montana, Wyoming, and Idaho. A later study of the Mountain region may find a change in the high levels of government spending and public services.

What does appear from region to region in this examination is not the power of a single explanation for regional peculiarities, but the power of regional norms to persist over time and to influence current styles in state politics and public services. The inclination toward large legislatures with at least one representative from each town and a reliance on locally raised taxes in New England can be traced to the seventeenth century, when locally oriented Congregationalists settled that region. Likewise in other regions, political imports brought by first settlers have remained to affect contemporary decisions. Yet the past may have only a limited influence on contemporary regional norms. Individual states and whole regions face continuing challenges to their traditions and occasionally make drastic changes in their political forms and practices. The Great Lakes states, for instance, became competitive politically in the face of industrialization, the immigration of Southerners, and the reawakening of Democratic parties. In the Northeast and on the Plains, Massachusetts, New York, New Jersey, and Nebraska have recently broken with tradition and enacted statewide sales taxes.

7

REGIONAL PATTERNS IN THE
POLICY-MAKING PROCESS:
THE CASE OF STATE
GOVERNMENT EXPENDITURES[1]

In previous chapters of this book we have examined regional scores on measures of state politics and public policy, and have weeded out those instances where economic characteristics account for the regional findings. Even after controlling for economic characteristics, we have found significant regional differences on most of our dependent variables. However, our analyses have not probed beneath the surface manifestations of state politics and policy. One feature we have overlooked is the interaction within each region of political and economic phenomena that influence the nature of policies.

In this chapter we shall look for regional peculiarities in the relationships between political-economic traits and state

[1] This chapter is adapted from the author's "Regional Patterns in the Expenditures of American States," *Western Political Quarterly*, XX (December 1967), 955–971.

government expenditures. We already know from Chapter 3 that the level of state expenditures varies from one region to another. Here we shall see if expenditures in each region respond differently to certain important elements of the environment. The language we shall use is borrowed from systems theory.[2] The relevant "outputs" of the state political system are government expenditures; the "inputs" represent social-economic needs, demands, and resources, as well as political structures, rules, and traditions that might influence officials who make expenditure decisions. The interactions between inputs and outputs are measured with statistical relationships between independent variables and state government expenditures. If our analyses are sensitive, these interactions should define the most important influences upon expenditures; when we search from region to region for how they differ, we will be looking for regional differences in the factors that affect government expenditures.

Techniques

The basic question of this chapter is: *Are there regional peculiarities in the patterns of interaction between state government expenditures and their determinants?* In order to answer this, it will be necessary to establish the nationwide pattern of interaction between state expenditures and their determinants, and then compare this to the patterns within each of several regions. In dealing with the question we shall employ a larger variety of expenditure measures than we have used in previous chapters, and 18 independent variables as likely determinants of state expenditures.

This chapter examines two types of state expenditure: general expenditures per capita, and general expenditures per $1,000 of personal income.[3] Although the states that score high in expenditures per capita also tend to score high in expenditures per $1,000 of personal income (Pearson's $r = .67$

[2] See David Easton, *A Framework for Political Analysis* (Englewood Cliffs, N.J.: Prentice-Hall, 1965).

[3] As defined by the U.S. Bureau of the Census, "general expenditures" include all spending except for state liquor stores and insurance trust funds.

for 1962), there is enough difference between the two measures to warrant considering them separately. "Expenditures per capita" is a measure of money spent in relation to the population being served by state programs. As such, it suggests how much each state is devoting to improving or maintaining the quantity or quality of its public services.[4] Expenditures per $1,000 of personal income is a measure of spending in relation to economic resources. States that make high expenditures per $1,000 of personal income appear to be showing a greater commitment of their resources to state affairs, and—assuming a universal reluctance of people to pay taxes—they appear to be making greater *economic and political efforts* in supporting the activities of state government. The following analysis will deal with expenditures in total, and expenditures for each major category of state operations: education, highways, public welfare, health and hospitals, natural resources (agriculture, forestry, fish and game, and recreation), public safety (police and corrections), and general government (legislative and judicial operations plus financial administration and administration of insurance trust funds). In each case, spending will be defined both as general expenditures per capita, and general expenditures per $1,000 of personal income. A comparison of means and coefficients of variability will indicate regional differences and the relative distinctiveness of each region with respect to the measures of state expenditures. Correlation and regression analysis are most often used to determine the factors associated with differences in government expenditures, but the small number of states in some of the regions precludes use of these techniques for each region. Instead, the expenditures and other characteristics of each region

[4] It is not possible to claim that expenditures per capita measures the quality or quantity of state-supported public services. The quality or quantity of state-supported public services seems to result from a variety of factors not simply reflected in current expenditures per capita. Among these factors are amounts previously spent in accumulating capital facilities, financial contributions from local, federal, or private sources that supplement state-supported programs, the nature of economies derived from operations of a certain magnitude, and the training and motivations of state officials. See my "Government Expenditures and Public Services in the American States," *American Political Science Review*, LXI (December 1967), 1066–1077.

will be compared to nationwide models of state expenditure processes that have been determined by means of step-wise regression and a 48-state sample.[5] To the extent that each region fits this national model, it will be apparent that state expenditures in the region react to the same characteristics that influence state expenditures generally.

The step-wise regression program considered 18 independent variables as having potential relationships with state expenditures. Four of the variables measure aspects of the *centralization* in state-local relationships:

(*a*) percentage of state and local general revenue allocated to the state government after tax collections and intergovernmental transfers, 1962

(*b*) percentage of state and local governments' general revenue originating at the state level prior to intergovernmental transfers, 1962

(*c*) percentage of state and local governments' general revenue originating from sources other than local governments prior to intergovernmental transfers, 1962

(*d*) percentage of local government general revenue received from the state government, 1962

Three of the independent variables measure aspects of *political-economic constraints* upon state expenditures:

[5] A step-wise regression program first selects the independent variable that shows the strongest relationship with the dependent variable (state expenditures). In subsequent steps, the program selects the independent variables that—when added to the regression formula ($Y = a + b_1 X_1 + b_2 X_2 + \ldots b_k X_k$)—will explain the greatest percentage of as yet unexplained variation in state expenditures. With the addition of each independent variable, the proportion of interstate variations in expenditures that is explained increases. The percentage of explained variation is indicated by the coefficient of multiple determination (R^2). But after the inclusion of the most powerful independent variables, subsequent additions provide little further explanation of interstate variations in expenditures. In this study, no further independent variables were added to the regression formulae when a new variable would fail to add 5 percent to the existing coefficient of multiple determination. The program used to compute the formulae is "Stepwise Regression," in BMD Biomedical Computer Programs (Health Sciences Computing Facility, University of California, Los Angeles, September 1, 1965), pp. 233 ff.

(*e*) previous expenditures (1957)[6]

(*f*) percentage of state general revenue received from the federal government, 1962

(*g*) "tax effort": percentage of per capita personal income paid by citizens to state and local governments in taxes, 1962

Six of the independent variables measure aspects of the *ease of citizen access to state government:*

(*h*) average percentage of voting-age citizens casting ballots in elections for state governor and U.S. senator during 1954 and 1958

(*i*) David-Eisenberg index of legislative apportionment

(*j*) Ranney index of two-party competition in state politics, 1946–1963 [7]

(*k*) incidence of local governments per 10,000 population, 1962

(*l*) average monthly salary of state employees, 1962

(*m*) number of state employees per 10,000 population, 1962

Five of the independent variables measure aspects of *economic development* in each state:

(*n*) per capita personal income, 1962

(*o*) population, 1962

(*p*) percentage of population living in urban areas, 1960

(*q*) percentage of employees working in manufacturing, 1958–1959

(*r*) value added by manufacturing, per capita, 1958

6 "Previous expenditures" will be in terms of per capita or per $1,000 of personal income, in total expenditures or in expenditures for a certain function in order to correspond with the nature of the dependent variable.

7 Austin Ranney, "Parties in State Politics," in Herbert Jacob and Kenneth N. Vines, *Politics in the American States* (Boston: Little, Brown, 1965), p. 65. The measure of competition equals the difference between each state's score on Ranney's index of Democratic-Republican strength in state politics, and .5000.

Several hypotheses guided the selection of independent variables for the step-wise regression of state government expenditures. The measures of state-local centralization assess the proportion of state and local government financial responsibilities assumed by state agencies. Where this proportion is high, state governments are taking charge of revenue and expenditure functions that are provided by local governments elsewhere. Presumably, a large state share of these functions will serve to increase total state expenditures. Therefore, there should be positive relationships between variables *a* through *d* and expenditures.

Previous expenditures, federal aid, and tax effort are "constraints" because officials who make expenditure decisions seem likely to be hemmed in or permitted flexibility according to the level of these variables. Previous expenditures provide the basis for budget decisions about pending operations. Budgeteers look first at their previous appropriations, and begin their calculations from the assumption that the governor and legislature will grant their "base" automatically. The larger the base, therefore, the larger the agency's request and the probable appropriation. Federal aids are constraints because the granting agencies require recipients to match the aid with a certain proportion of state resources. Moreover, the grant itself forms part of the agency's budget base, and adds to the security with which administrators face the legislature. Tax effort is a constraint because of the widespread reluctance of state officials to borrow, and because the constitutional restrictions against indebtedness require that populations be willing to support high spending levels with high taxes. It is expected that variables *e* through *g* will show positive relationships with state government expenditures.

The ease of citizen access to state government seems likely to increase with voter turnout, the equity of legislative apportionment, the degree of two-party competition, the incidence of local governments, and the size and quality of the state's administrative corps. With high voter turnout, the population seems best prepared to have its views penetrate government circles; with equitable legislative apportionment, urban and rural voters are most likely to have a fair opportunity to influence the legislature; with intense party competition, citizens are most likely to find politicians willing to promote their interests in exchange for electoral support; with a high incidence of local governments, state agencies should feel the greatest pressures to assist municipalities, counties, and school districts; and a large and well-paid body of professional administrators seems most likely to be familiar with new developments in public services and aware of citizens' needs and demands. Some of the literature cited in Appendix A suggests that citizen access is likely to stimulate high levels of government expenditures and public services. For this reason, the initial hypotheses predicted positive relationships between variables h through m and the state expenditures.

States that are well developed economically should be wealthy, urban, industrial states with large populations. Some existing literature suggests that these traits correspond with high levels of service demands upon governments and high levels of taxable resources, but *low* levels of state government expenditures per capita (see pages 105-110). And because well-to-do populations might support high expenditures with low economic effort, negative relationships were predicted between variables n through r and both state expenditures per capita and expenditures per \$1,000 of personal income.

The regression formulae of Table 7–1 indicate the independent variables that contribute most to the explanation of interstate variations in total expenditures, and expenditures for each major category of state operations. The formulae show the independent variables in the order of their selection by the step-wise program; that is, the most powerful independent variables follow immediately after the constants.

The characteristics that exert the strongest influences upon state expenditures are the political-economic constraints on expenditures and the degree of centralization in state-local relationships. In every formula, the most powerful independent variable is either previous expenditures or federal aid. With respect to total expenditures (both per capita and per \$1,000 of personal income), second in importance is the percentage of state-local revenue originating from non-local sources. Our measures of citizen access to state government

TABLE 7–1. REGRESSION FORMULAE RELEVANT TO STATE GOVERNMENT EXPENDITURES: COMPUTED WITH 48 STATES

DEPENDENT VARIABLE *	CON-STANT	INDEPENDENT VARIABLES OF DECREASING STRENGTH **	COEFFICIENTS OF MULTIPLE DETERMINATION	
			Obtained with Independent Variables Noted	Obtained with All 18 Independent Variables
Total Exp/Cap	$= -.66 +$	$.88(e) + 1.05(c)$	.78	.95
Educ Exp/Cap	$= 10.00 +$	$1.27(e)$	.88	.94
Highways Exp/Cap	$= -22.47 +$	$1.86(f) + .64(e)$	.72	.91
Pub Welf Exp/Cap	$= 5.23 +$	$1.04(e)$	.87	.93
Health–Hos Exp/Cap	$= 3.96 +$	$.78(e)$	.72	.82
Nat Res Exp/Cap	$= -4.37 +$	$.43(e) + .17(f) + .04(m)$	.79	.85
Pub Safe Exp/Cap	$= -9.43 +$	$.23(e) + .0172(l) - .00015(p) + .00186(n) + .06(c)$	.78	.90
Genl Govt Exp/Cap	$= .48 +$	$1.26(e)$	.92	.97
Total Exp/$	$= -89.51 +$	$.38(e) + 1.33(c) + 7.10(g)$	.89	.96
Educ Exp/$	$= 2.99 +$	$1.14(e) +$	.89	.94
Highways Exp/$	$= -32.77 +$	$.90(f) + .39(a) + 1.85(g)$	.81	.91
Pub Welf Exp/$	$= 1.49 +$	$.98(e)$	.90	.95
Health–Hos Exp/$	$= 2.95 +$	$.70(e) - .03(h)$	.63	.77
Nat Res Exp/$	$= -1.09 +$	$.49(e) + .10(f)$	.78	.86
Pub Safe Exp/$	$= -.86 +$	$.49(e) + .00726(l) - .00006(o) - .01(h)$	.68	.84
Genl Govt Exp/$	$= .22 +$	$1.06(e)$	.88	.95

*The dependent variables are expenditures per capita and expenditures per $1,000 of personal income.
**The independent variables are designated by the letters associated with them in the text above.

and economic development played minor roles with respect to 1962 state expenditures.

By means of the regression formulae from Table 7–1, it is possible to determine the extent to which average expenditures of states in a region relate to the same factors that affect the expenditures of states generally. By substituting for the independent variables of the formulae the values associated with the average characteristics of states in a region, we arrive at formulae which will estimate the average state expenditures in the region. The ratio between the estimated value and the real value of the expenditures will indicate the correspondence between state expenditure processes throughout the United States. The further removed this ratio is from 1.00 (obtained where the expenditures estimated on the basis of a 48-state regression model equal the real expenditures of states in the region), the more distinct will be the state expenditure processes in the region.

This chapter employs the 14 regional groupings used in the analysis of covariance reported in Chapter 5, plus another regional grouping used for the first time in this chapter: a group of seven contiguous states whose expenditures were consistently low. On both expenditures per capita and expenditures per $1,000 of personal income, these states score consistently in the lowest quartile. They are New Jersey, Pennsylvania, Ohio, Indiana, Illinois, Missouri, and Nebraska. The other regions considered in this chapter are identified on Table 7–2.

Regional Variations in State Expenditures

There are clear regional variations in the expenditures of American states, as is evident from the data of Table 7–2, which shows the average expenditures of states in each region as a percentage of average state expenditures over the nation as a whole.

In general, Northern and Eastern regions (including states north of the Ohio River and east of the Rockies) score low on expenditures. In expenditures per capita, it is only in education and natural resources that these regions tend to score at

TABLE 7–2. MEAN EXPENDITURES OF STATES IN EACH REGION AS A

REGION		EXPENDITURES/CAPITA						
	Total	Edu-ca-tion	High-ways	Pub-lic Wel-fare	Health–Hospi-tals	Na-tural Re-sources	Pub-lic Safety	Gen-eral Gov-ern-ment
North	.93	.82	.92	.88	1.25	.74	1.11	1.07
New England	.99	.65	1.12	1.05	1.40	.99	1.24	1.31
Mid-Atlantic *north*	.95	.99	.75	.73	1.40	.58	1.15	2.86
Great Lakes *and*	.85	.84	.87	.81	.91	.59	.93	.73
Northeast *east*	.93	.69	.95	.95	1.35	.85	1.13	1.23
Northcentral	.89	.83	.98	.88	.94	.84	.88	.73
Plains	.92	.82	1.07	.92	.95	1.01	.85	.75
Transmississippi	1.10	1.16	1.16	1.09	.87	1.31	1.08	1.09
Mountains *west*	1.18	1.24	1.47	1.00	.84	1.76	1.07	1.25
Far West	1.33	1.46	1.15	1.23	1.00	1.71	1.71	1.59
Transplains	1.24	1.40	1.27	1.09	.85	1.63	1.30	1.40
Southwest	1.08	1.33	.93	1.34	.64	.87	.84	1.03
Southeast *south*	.92	.98	.84	1.02	.89	.83	.72	.76
South	.96	1.03	.86	1.06	.96	.78	.81	1.19
7 States from New Jersey to Nebraska	.73	.67	.79	.84	.89	.60	.81	.72

least 15 percent below the national average; but this finding gains importance from the fact that spending for these functions averages 37 percent of total state expenditures per capita. In expenditures per \$1,000 of personal income, Northern and Eastern regions tend to score at least 15 percent below the national average in total expenditures and in expenditures for education, highways, public welfare, and natural resources. All of the Southern regions (South, Southeast, and Southwest) score high in expenditures per \$1,000 of personal income, es-

PERCENTAGE OF NATIONAL MEANS

EXPENDITURES/$1,000 OF PERSONAL INCOME

Total	Educa-tion	Highways	Public Welfare	Health–Hospitals	Natural Resources	Public Safety	General Govern-ment
.80	.69	.82	.74	1.09	.66	1.00	.94
.92	.61	1.07	.94	1.30	.96	1.18	1.22
.72	.75	.58	.56	1.11	.44	.92	.89
.75	.74	.76	.68	.81	.52	.86	.65
.82	.61	.87	.82	1.22	.79	1.03	1.10
.83	.76	.92	.79	.88	.78	.85	.69
.89	.78	1.03	.86	.93	.97	.85	.72
1.05	1.09	1.09	1.02	.84	1.23	1.03	1.05
1.17	1.20	1.42	.95	.41	1.71	1.08	1.24
1.04	1.16	.90	.97	.82	1.36	1.39	.78
1.16	1.29	1.17	.98	.79	1.49	1.21	1.31
1.19	1.45	1.00	1.45	.71	.96	.95	1.15
1.18	1.26	1.09	1.31	1.16	1.07	.95	.99
1.12	1.20	1.02	1.27	1.12	.94	.95	.96
.63	.58	.69	.71	.79	.51	.73	.64

pecially in the fields of education and public welfare. Yet in the fields that account for the bulk of state spending per capita (education, highways, public welfare, and health-hospitals), Southern regions show no consistent deviations from national averages. Western regions (Transplains, Mountain, Far West, Transmississippi, and Southwest) score high in both expenditures per $1,000 and expenditures per capita, especially in the fields of education, highways, and natural resources. The Western regions score low only in health and hospital expenditures.

Regional Similarities in State Expenditure Processes

The information in Table 7–3 helps to explain the regional differences in expenditures described above, and indicates the degree to which average state expenditures in each region relate to the factors that are related to state expenditures throughout the nation. It shows the ratios between estimated regional expenditures (based on the regression formulae of Table 7–1) and the actual expenditures of states in the 15 regions.

It appears that expenditures in the various regions respond to the same set of factors that influence state expenditures

TABLE 7–3. RATIOS OF REGIONAL MEAN EXPENDITURES ESTIMATED FROM

REGION	EXPENDITURES/CAPITA							
	Total	Educa-tion	High-ways	Public Welfare	Health–Hos-pitals	Natural Re-sources	Public Safety	General Govern-ment
North	1.01	1.03	.92	.92	.98	1.02	1.03	1.01
New England	1.01	.98	1.04	.93	.97	1.07	1.00	1.00
Mid-Atlantic	1.00	1.04	.76	.94	.90	.92	1.07	.99
Great Lakes	1.00	1.07	.87	.89	1.11	1.00	1.00	1.04
Northeast	1.00	.97	1.02	.92	.92	.97	1.03	.98
Northcentral	.99	1.07	.98	1.01	1.04	1.11	1.03	1.06
Plains	.99	1.03	1.06	1.03	1.01	1.08	1.04	1.00
Transmississippi	.98	.97	1.02	1.05	1.07	1.01	1.02	1.00
Mountains	.94	.91	.95	1.19	1.02	.94	1.10	.96
Far West	.93	.94	.96	.96	1.07	.88	.92	.99
Transplains	.96	.93	1.01	1.09	1.06	.95	1.02	.99
Southwest	1.08	1.01	1.12	1.00	1.28	1.31	1.07	1.08
Southeast	1.04	1.03	1.07	1.00	.93	1.07	1.00	1.00
South	1.05	1.02	1.02	.98	.97	.98	1.00	.98
7 States from New Jersey to Nebraska	1.03	1.12	1.01	.97	1.06	1.04	1.04	1.08

throughout the nation. In no case do the total expenditures of a region vary by more than 8 percent from those estimated by the 48-state regression formulae. There are several instances of greater variation from the national patterns in expenditures for certain functions, but the incidence of these cases is not high. Of the 210 relevant cells in Table 7–3, there are only 24 in which real expenditures vary from predicted expenditures by more than 10 percent, and only in 12 of these do the real expenditures vary from predicted expenditures by more than 15 percent.

Nationwide, the characteristics related to high expenditures per capita are high previous expenditures per capita and

48-STATE REGRESSION FORMULAE TO ACTUAL REGIONAL MEAN EXPENDITURES

				EXPENDITURES/$1,000 OF PERSONAL INCOME			
Total	*Educa-tion*	*Highways*	*Public Welfare*	*Health– Hospitals*	*Natural Resources*	*Public Safety*	*General Govern-ment*
1.02	.99	.92	.91	.95	.98	1.00	.99
1.02	.93	1.03	.94	.93	.96	1.00	.99
1.05	1.03	.80	.92	.91	.89	1.02	.96
.98	1.03	.82	.86	1.06	1.09	.92	1.01
1.00	1.02	1.02	.93	.97	1.17	1.03	1.00
1.01	1.05	.96	.98	1.05	1.06	.99	1.02
1.01	1.10	1.06	1.10	1.03	1.12	1.04	1.09
1.00	.98	1.09	1.07	1.05	1.02	.98	1.01
.97	.91	.99	1.21	.76	.91	1.00	.96
1.00	.97	1.05	1.00	1.10	.95	.89	1.01
.99	.93	1.01	1.08	1.10	.95	.97	.99
1.04	.96	1.09	.98	1.26	1.18	1.02	1.01
.97	1.02	.99	.98	.96	.97	1.00	.99
1.00	1.03	1.03	.99	.93	1.11	.99	1.00
.94	1.10	1.04	.98	1.03	1.20	.99	1.05

state-local centralization. The factors related to high expenditures per $1,000 of personal income are high previous ex-
penditures per $1,000 of personal income, a high degree of
state-local centralization, and a high percentage of citizens' personal income taken in taxes. Table 7–4 verifies that differences
on these characteristics distinguish the high spending regions
from the low spending regions. The table shows averages on
the critical variables for regions scoring at least 15 percent
above or below national averages of state expenditures. In
every case, high spending regions are above low spending regions on previous expenditures and the percentage of state-
local revenues originating at non-local sources. In the case of
tax effort, there is only one region (Southeast) that scores high
on expenditures per $1,000 of personal income but is not also
above the low spenders on this critical independent variable.

Table 7–4 also indicates that high spending and low spending regions have adhered to their expenditure patterns for
many years. It adds further credence to the finding that previous expenditures exert considerable influence upon current
spending. In every case but one (the Mountain region in
1929), the high spending regions of 1962 were above the national average in both 1947 and 1929, and each of the regions
that were low spenders in 1962 was below the national average
in 1947 and 1929.

Summary

This chapter provides evidence for three propositions:

1. The characteristics that show the strongest relationships
with state expenditures are measures of political-economic
constraints on expenditures (especially previous expenditures)
and measures of state-local centralization. The addition of
economic-development measures, or measures of citizen access,
makes little further contribution to the explanation of state
expenditures.

2. There are distinct regional variations in the expenditures
of American states. In general, Western states are high
spenders, and Northern and Eastern states are low spenders.
Southern states are not distinctive in expenditures per capita,

TABLE 7–4. MEANS ON CRITICAL CHARACTERISTICS FOR REGIONS SCORING 15 PERCENT ABOVE OR BELOW 48-STATE MEANS ON EXPENDITURES

	EXPENDITURES/CAPITA			
Previous Expenditures	1957	1947	1929	State-Local Revenue from Non-Local Sources
Low-Scoring Regions				
Great Lakes	$116.36	$56.57	$15.57	50.5%
7 States from New Jersey to Nebraska	98.79	50.12	17.87	48.0
48-STATE MEAN	136.64	63.09	20.61	59.3
High-Scoring Regions				
Mountain	157.63	77.55	22.98	60.7
Transplains	172.21	85.59	25.81	62.0
Far West	184.19	91.98	28.80	59.8

	EXPENDITURES/$1,000 PERSONAL INCOME				
Previous Expenditures	1957	1947	1929	State-Local Revenue from Non-Local Sources	Tax Effort
Low-Scoring Regions					
North	$ 58.69	$36.33	$27.07	53.6%	9.2%
Mid-Atlantic	52.38	30.08	24.52	54.8	8.6
Great Lakes	53.02	35.03	20.08	50.5	9.1
Northeast	60.17	37.58	29.63	52.1	9.5
Northcentral	64.45	36.14	29.11	51.5	9.5
7 States from New Jersey to Nebraska	45.55	29.98	19.92	48.0	8.3
48-STATE MEAN	74.10	45.44	35.69	59.3	9.5
High-Scoring Regions					
Mountain	82.27	51.52	35.65	60.7	10.5
Transplains	85.07	54.51	40.47	62.0	10.2
Southwest	92.40	65.04	44.07	66.7	9.9
Southeast	84.34	53.11	42.91	67.6	9.1

but they score high in expenditures per $1,000 of personal income.

3. Regional patterns in expenditures do not result from unique regional political processes. Rather, regional spending peculiarities are consistent in reflecting the influence of political-economic constraints and of state-local centralization on expenditures. These characteristics are generally influential with respect to state expenditures. Thus, there are regional peculiarities in certain *outputs of government* (current expenditures), in *political-economic constraints upon government officials* (previous expenditures, tax effort, and federal aid), and in *state government structure* (state-local centralization). But regional peculiarities extend only so far. The relative importance of the characteristics that seem to exert great influence on the expenditures of state governments are similar from region to region. This finding points to an important national similarity in the political processes of state governments.

APPENDIXES

APPENDIX A

THE LITERATURES OF
REGIONALISM AND COMPARATIVE
STATE POLITICS

Different Designations of "Region"

The literature on regionalism reveals at least four principal types of designations for the term "region." In one sense, the region is a *natural area* that is made distinct by geographical, climatic, or agricultural features: a river valley; a mountain range; the peculiar combinations of soil, terrain, and climate that produce the corn belt, the wheat belt, or the cotton belt.

A second principal type of region is the *economic region*. This typically centers around the industrial-commercial-financial-cultural resources of a metropolitan area, and includes within it the middle- and small-sized cities and rural areas that provide the market area for the metropolis. The specific borders of the region may vary with the indicator that is used to define them—the circulation patterns of large-city newspapers, the territory served by the city's wholesalers, the area from which daily commuters come to work in the city. These may be multiple special-purpose regions having similar but not identical borders. Their common focus will be the metropolitan city, however, and their common feature will be the economic intercourse that is focused on that city.

A third type of region is that area which supports loyalties, patriotism, self-identification, and cultural folkways. In this country the distinctive *cultural regions* include the Old South, New England, and the Southwest. The traits of regional citizens are peculiarities of speech and dress, views about morality or politics, or a distinctive ethnic heritage. This type of region is often more clearly established in the minds of its residents than on any map. The cultural regions are broad areas that include individuals and communities that differ from the cultural mainstream. In the Old South, for example, mountaineers differ in speech and politics from lowland whites who live in areas where plantations thrived; the whites in the Piedmont textile cities differ from both of these types; and the Negroes differ from all three. In New England there are sharp cultural differences between communities where "Yankees" still dominate and the larger cities of southern New England where Catholic immigrants from all corners of Europe outnumber—and outvote—the Anglo-Saxon Protestants. In the Southwest the sharpest contrast is between Anglos and Latins. Despite these differences within states or communities, the cultural type of region is that which most frequently may come to the minds of political observers and participants, and which may have the most to do with how people think and behave with respect to public affairs.

Fourth, there is the *administrative region:* that which is contrived by federal agencies to facilitate the administration of their services, or by large private firms for the convenience of their sales force. States, too, divide themselves for governmental purposes. Presumably, regional offices make officials of governments or private firms more accessible to their clients and facilitate the adjustment of services to local needs. These administrative regions often coincide with regions of the other types; for example, most agencies of the federal government have a southern region with an office in Atlanta. However, some agencies employ cultural criteria in designing their regions, while others employ the natural or economic conceptions of regions. The result is that boundaries of administrative regions vary considerably with the nature of the service and with the agency that is responsible for its administration.

Regionalism and Sectionalism

In some of the literature on regionalism there is an insistence that "regions" are not the same as "sections." Although the use of terms is not consistent from one author to the next, it is clear that there are two distinct phenomena, whose contrast is often highlighted by those who urge political or administrative reforms along regional lines. "Sections" and "sectionalism" are viewed as the sharp divisions that separate political-economic cultures and set one section against others. "Regions" and "regionalism," in contrast, are often viewed as providing an opportunity to plan and provide public services in the context of the peculiar needs generated by an area, and to integrate the services of that area (or region) into the goals of the larger nation. In brief, sectionalism is seen as the nucleus of inter-area antagonism that is centered around the defense of an area's culture or economy against the larger national interest; the example most often analyzed by historians is the sectionalism that has set the South against other sections of the country. Regionalism, on the other hand, is portrayed as the effort to meet an area's needs in such a way as to integrate the area into the national culture and economy. The work of the Tennessee Valley Authority is the best example of "regionalism" carried to fruition. The TVA has provided the area drained by the Tennessee River with the economic wherewithal to enjoy the benefits of American culture, and the life-styles of the area's residents have changed accordingly.[1]

1 For a classic work on regionalism, see Howard W. Odum and Harry Estell Moore, *American Regionalism: A Cultural-Historical Approach to National Integration* (New York: Henry Holt, 1938); for a discussion of regionalism as it is useful for government administration and public planning, see Marshall E. Dimock, "Political and Administrative Aspects of Regional Planning," in *Planning for City, State, Region, and Nation,* Proceedings of the Joint Conference on Planning, 1936. For a discussion of regionalism *vs.* sectionalism, see Odum and Moore, *op. cit.,* pp. 35–51; and Daniel J. Elazar, *American Federalism: A View From the States* (New York: Thomas Y. Crowell, 1966), pp. 112 ff.

In this book we do not enter any debate about the benefits to be derived from the perspective of regional planning or service-administration and we do not lament the persistence of sectional cleavages. Our efforts are in the direction of description and analysis rather than advocacy. To be sure, our findings may have relevance for those who concern themselves with the issues of sectionalism and regional planning, but we have made the inquiry without any emotional investment in our findings. We employ the term "region" instead of "section" in order to avoid the implication that our areas necessarily manifest deep-seated attitudes or behaviors that serve to perpetuate their separateness. Indeed, one of our concerns is to determine *how uniform* and *how long-lasting* are the features of politics and public policy in each of the areas that we consider. "Region" appears to be a term that is less encumbered with value-charged connotations than "section," and so it serves better our scientific aspirations. We expected to find several traits that are deeply embedded in the history of certain regions, but we were prepared also to discover that state politics and policy have been subject to considerable variations within regions during a recent period of time, and that they experienced considerable variation over time. While some areas of the country are becoming less distinctive in their regional traits, other areas are becoming more so. In this book, "regionalism" refers to resemblances in politics and policy that are apparent among neighboring states—resemblances which may or may not be growing or diminishing in importance, and may or may not lend themselves to "regionally"-oriented administrative schemes.

Studies of Regions by Political Scientists

The portion of the "regional literature" to which this book relates most closely is that produced by political scientists who have described the politics of individual regions. Key's classic study of Southern politics [2] has set the mold for this body of research. Indeed, a number of his former graduate students

[2] V. O. Key, *Southern Politics: In State and Nation* (New York: Alfred A. Knopf, 1949).

have made the most important contributions to our knowledge of regional politics: Duane Lockard's book on New England,[3] John Fenton's works on politics in the Border states and the Midwest,[4] and the articles of Frank Munger [5] are written in the style that was established by their former professor.

Although this group of scholars has dominated the regional literature, they are not alone. Thomas Donnelly's *Rocky Mountain Politics* [6] and Frank Jonas' *Western Politics* [7] must also be considered in any review of the literature. Characteristically, each of these studies has been limited in the scope of political activities considered, and they have neglected to make systematic comparisons between their own region and the remainder of the country (we shall examine these shortcomings below). But no matter what we say about the problems inherent in the existing descriptions of the politics in American regions, these findings characterize much of what is believed—and taught—about regional variations in American politics. As it is summarized here, the descriptive material is presented in the regional boundaries that are employed in existing literature. However, it is one task of this book to compare these traditional boundaries with several others that may divide each group of states from the others. Another task is to identify in a precise fashion the prominent traits of each region, and to identify those which can—and cannot—be explained by reference to the current level of economic development.

The Northeast

The Northeast has been defined to include the states north of Washington, D.C., and east of the Great Lakes. The re-

[3] Duane Lockard, *New England State Politics* (Princeton: Princeton University Press, 1959).

[4] John Fenton, *Politics in the Border States* (New Orleans: The Hauser Press, 1956); and *Midwest Politics* (New York: Holt, Rinehart and Winston, 1966).

[5] Frank Munger, *American State Politics: Readings for Comparative Analysis* (New York: Thomas Y. Crowell, 1966); and Frank Munger, "Two-Party Politics in Indiana" (unpublished Ph.D. dissertation, Harvard University, 1955).

[6] Albuquerque: University of New Mexico Press, 1940.

[7] Salt Lake City: University of Utah Press, 1961.

gional frontiers extend to Maryland, Delaware, and West Virginia on the south, and the Great Lakes in the west. Depending upon one's focus, each of several bordering states may be included or excluded from the region. Although no systematic study claims to encompass the politics of the Northeast as such, Duane Lockard has examined the politics of the New England states and other authors have either examined individual states in the region or have made casual generalizations about politics throughout the region.[8] As in other regions, Northeastern politics show significant intra-regional differences. Even in tiny New England there are dissimilarities between states in the north and in the south. All New England shares certain common characteristics: early settlement; a common ethnic-religious background; state constitutions that are relatively old, brief, and simple; a tendency to administer locally many programs that in other regions are handled by state agencies; large state legislatures that typically include at least one representative from each town; and the primacy of the town meeting in rural areas. Yet Maine, New Hampshire, and Vermont remain relatively rural, Yankee, Protestant, and Republican, while in Massachusetts, Rhode Island, and Connecticut the Yankee ascendency has long been replaced by the Democratic descendants of Catholic immigrants from Ireland and from southern and eastern Europe. The ethnic infusion of the New England population has had significant impacts on the electoral process. Professional politicians identify one another and their candidates in ethnic terms, and seek to balance party tickets with a proper representative of each main ethnic group. In some cases certain places on the ticket are considered the legitimate possession of an ethnic group. For many years the Democratic nominee for Connecticut's at-large Congressional seat "had to be" a Pole, and one Portuguese after another succeeded to the office of Registrar of Voters in Fall River, Massachusetts. Lockard finds the ethnic fixation of New England politicians to be as prominent as the racial fixation of Southern politicians. In both regions there is a tendency to make electoral appeals based not on policy issues but on one's emotional identification with one's culture.

8 See Munger, *American State Politics,* pp. 105–206.

Not only does ethnicity divide politicians in the Northeast, but the related Catholic-Protestant division also has an impact on politics. In Massachusetts and Connecticut, birth control legislation imposed by Victorian Protestants in the nineteenth century has recently provoked antagonism between Catholics (who now support the anti-birth control legislation) and the Protestants, Jews, and other non-Catholics who are in the opposition. Many school children in the Northeast attend Catholic parochial schools, and the public support of parochial education is another source of political friction. In Rhode Island, New Hampshire, Pennsylvania, New York, Massachusetts, and New Jersey, over twenty percent of the elementary and secondary pupils attend non-public schools. While Catholic leaders argue that public school funds should supplement the private support given to parochial schools, non-Catholics complain that parochial school enrollments serve to lessen the support given to public school budgets.

Although it is only the most Northeasterly of the states that show a pervasive concern with religious and ethnic issues, much of the larger region shows the traits of intense inter-party competition (urban Democrats against suburban and rural Republicans), and considerable local government autonomy and self-support. The localistic tendencies stretch to the western edges of the Northeast region more perfectly than they extend to the southern border. State agencies in Delaware and Maryland are more like Southern states in their exercise of authority that belongs to local government in the North.

The South

Even though the South as a region is considered to be highly distinct, culturally and politically, authors have given varying definitions of its geographical outline. V. O. Key, for example, defines the South simply as those states that seceded from the Union to form the Confederacy: Virginia, North Carolina, South Carolina, Tennessee, Georgia, Alabama, Florida, Mississippi, Arkansas, Louisiana, and Texas. Others combine this region with some or all of the "Border states"— Delaware, Maryland, West Virginia, Kentucky, Missouri, and

Oklahoma [9]—which are akin to the South because they received much of their initial population from there, attempted to secede from the Union (the stars of Kentucky and Missouri are included in the Confederacy's flag), or legislated statewide racial segregation of public education.

There are significant economic, social, and political differences among such "Southern" states as Delaware, West Virginia, Arkansas, Florida, Mississippi, and Texas. But each state of the South shows at least some of the following characteristics: widespread poverty; low levels of popular education; a large population of nonwhites who have felt the cultural and political disadvantages of slavery and segregation; low levels of participation in politics (by both whites and nonwhites); widespread conservatism, both social and political; one-party politics; governors who are strong politically if not constitutionally; and a relative centralization of state-local government relationships.

The economic and cultural poverty of the South reveals itself in low levels of personal income per capita, low scores on adult attainment of education, low levels of literacy, and a high incidence of selective service inductees who fail the mental examination. Few Southern universities or libraries have attained national recognition. The economic and cultural problem of the South is based on a poor-soil rural economy and low-capital, low-wage industry that has developed there during the twentieth century. With the labor surplus and the historically exploited minority, wages in the South are typically lower than they are for similar jobs elsewhere in the country.

One-party domination of state and local politics in the South has meant that factions of the Democratic party have done battle with one another. In some states these factions have attained a permanence not unlike that of organized parties: Long and anti-Long factions in Louisiana and Byrd and anti-Byrd politicians in Virginia have taken party-like positions against one another for many years. In other Southern states, factions have been more temporary in their identification with transient political figures. The principal disadvan-

[9] See note 4 above.

tage that is claimed for factional politics is the lack of predictability. In the absence of permanently organized political parties whose positions in any one year resemble those taken in earlier years, the voter is hard pressed to identify his vote for one candidate or another with the services he would be likely to receive with their election. Furthermore, the elected legislator holding a seat in a one-party state lacks the cues that policy-relevant parties might provide to help him vote on a piece of legislation. Partly because of the absence of a well-organized partisan opposition, Southern governors have attained considerable political strength. Robert Highsaw describes the Southern governor as being almost solely in control of the resources that can attract support from a group of legislators: government jobs, roads, improvements at the state institutions within a legislator's district, and government purchasing. Despite constitutional prohibitions against serving consecutive terms and an enforced sharing of formal decision-making powers (such as Florida's "cabinet" system of shared executive power), Southern governors have exploited their positions in order to develop command of their legislatures.[10]

The position of the Southern governor is enhanced further by the historic centralization of government in Southern states. The colonial South differed from the North by lacking a population sufficient to develop numerous small towns, nor did Southern settlers have the religious inclination of New England Congregationalists to nurture locally autonomous units. Also, the poverty of the South has worked in favor of centralization at the state level. Many municipal and county governments in the South do not have sufficient economic resources within their jurisdiction to support their needs for public service. And the tax on real property that is constitutionally available to local governments is not one that works well in poverty. With depression, the value of real property is low, as is the capacity of individual property owners to pay large sums of money to the government. In contrast, the state-collected sales tax has remained productive in a depressed situation as people continue to make retail purchases in at

---

[10] Robert Highsaw, "The Southern Governor: Challenge to the Strong Governor Theme," *Public Administration Review*, XIX (1959), 7–11.

least small amounts; likewise, state income taxes that have withholding provisions take revenue from wage earners in tolerably small amounts as they receive their salaries. Moreover, state taxes have access to the economy of their entire jurisdiction and can draw wealth from urban areas in order to help support programs in poor rural counties. Because Southern states are inclined by history and economics to pay for and provide services that local governments provide elsewhere, Southern governors and other state officials have a great deal to say about the salary of schoolteachers, the location of new or improved roads, and public medical facilities.

Within the South, two sub-regions—the mountain area of the Appalachians in the east and the Ozarks in the west—share or surpass the low wages, low training, and low industrialization that occurs generally in the South, but do not share the high incidence of nonwhites or a Democratic party loyalty. The poorest county in the state of Georgia, for example, is Union County, which lies in the far northern section of the state on the North Carolina border; in 1960 its per capita personal income was $646, none of its 6,500 residents lived in an urban area, its population change between 1950 and 1960 was minus 11.0 percent, and it had no recorded nonwhite residents. On three occasions between 1924 and 1964, Union County supported Republican presidential candidates: it gave 55 percent of its votes to Warren Harding in 1920, 82 percent to Herbert Hoover in 1928, and 57 percent to Richard Nixon in 1960. On four other occasions (1924, 1948, 1952, and 1956), at least 45 percent of Union County's voters cast for Republican candidates. During this entire period, the state of Georgia gave a majority to only one Republican candidate (Goldwater) and failed to give any other Republican even 40 percent of its vote.

The conservatism of Southern politicians has never been universal. The antebellum period saw many Southerners who opposed the institution of slavery, and the period immediately preceding the 1860 election saw significant opposition to secession in most Southern states. In recent years, white Southerners have been leaders in the struggle for racial equality. Ralph McGill, Eugene Patterson, Harry Golden, and Hodding Carter have won national recognition for their journalistic efforts in behalf of social progress, and Atlanta's mayor Ivan Allan testified before Congress in behalf of the public accommodations section of the 1964 Civil Rights Act. But along with these liberals (who must be called "moderates" in the parlance of Southern politics) there remain George Wallace, Ross Barnett, and Strom Thurmond as representatives of the strong conservative strain in the region's politics.

Although there have been Republican strongholds in the mountain areas of the Southern states since the Civil War, and a newly developing Republicanism in the cities and suburbs during the 1950's and 1960's, state and local politics in the South remain heavily Democratic. As late as 1964, only 87 Republicans were sitting in the state legislature of the eleven former Confederate states, and two states (Mississippi and South Carolina) had no Republican legislators. Tennessee had the largest Republican delegations: 25 percent of the lower house and 33 percent of the upper house. However, the heavy Democratic majorities in Southern state politics no longer extend to the presidential level. The solid Democratic support shook in 1928, tremored in 1948, and now is hardly a probability in Presidential elections as the national Democratic party has moved away from positions that the mass of Southerners will tolerate. And increasingly, the Southern "presidential Republicans" have expressed their party allegiance in state and local elections. Florida elected a Republican governor in 1966, and voters in many Southern states returned record numbers of post-Reconstruction Republicans to the state legislatures. If this trend toward increased Republicanism in state governments continues, it may reflect or precede other profound changes in Southern politics.

The West

Like other regions, the West is variously defined. Although a common demarcation begins at the eastern borders of Montana, Wyoming, Colorado, and New Mexico, some conceptions of the West have included states as far east as the Mississippi River. Within this larger region, the Plains states, Rocky

Mountain states, and the Pacific coastal states have been treated as sub-regions in themselves.[11]

It is said that much of the politics that is "typically Western" results from topographic or economic peculiarities such as population diffusion, huge empty spaces, uneven land surface, mineral resources, and the uneven distribution of water resources. Out of these features has come a pervasive concern for transportation and resource development, particularly the development of water resources. Another politically significant characteristic of the West is the high incidence of federal land ownership. Whereas there is no state east of the Rocky Mountains in which the federal government owns more than 13 percent of the land, in no state west of this line does it own less than 29 percent. And several Western states approach Nevada's level of federal land ownership: 86 percent of the area. Although much of the federal land has limited economic potential, its ownership is a source of contention for Western politicians. Because of the established principle that federal ownership (even of marginal lands) within a state carries federal responsibilities for economic assistance to the state government, and because Western states score low on personal income and industrialization, the development of the region has been dependent upon federal aid. Western states score highest in their proportionate use of federal money. As recently as 1958, eight of the eleven Westernmost states enjoyed more federal expenditures (including federal aid) within their borders than they paid in federal taxes.[12]

In party competition and voter turnout, Western states score higher than any other region. In part, intense party competition reflects the recent settlement of the West. By far the greatest intra-national migration occurred after the Civil War and settled the West with both Northerners and Southerners. Since that time there has been no party-affecting trauma approaching the magnitude of the Civil War that has been able to align Westerners generally into one party or another. Along with inter-party competition, the West has rather weak party organizations. This is noticed in the use of

11 See the works of Donnelly, Jonas, and Munger cited above.
12 Jonas, *op. cit.*, p. 4.

popular electoral devices: referendum and recall provisions; Washington's "blanket primary" that permits a voter to select candidates in both parties at the same time; the now-repealed California statute that allowed a candidate to file in the primary of both parties; and the extra-party "Democratic clubs" of California. Thus, the West exhibits weak party organizations along with strong party competition, whereas the South demonstrates weak party organizations in the presence of little party competition. At least in these cases, regional peculiarities appear to be more important than general principles of party organization and competition.

Some peculiar traits of the West have divided its subregions against one another. While all the Western states have a strong interest in water resource development, they oppose one another in the selection of sites for development and the definition of formulae for water distribution. Nevada and California, for example, have aligned themselves against Arizona for use of the Colorado River flow. And while the coastal states of Washington and California reap great economic benefits from defense contracts, other Western states have urged that federal agencies distribute government contracts partly on the basis of economic needs.

The Middle West

The Middle West is defined loosely as the region that is left over after the remaining states are assigned to the Northeast, South, or West.[13] From the eastern boundary of Ohio the region extends to the eastern or western borders of the Dakotas, Nebraska, and Kansas (depending on whether one views the Plains States as being "Western" or "Middle Western"). From the Canadian border on the north the Middle West goes southward to the Ohio River in the east and to the Kansas-Oklahoma (or Oklahoma-Texas) line in the west. Topographically the area is flat, and economically it supports a combination of industry and agriculture. Generally speaking, an urban, industrial, Democratic concentration decreases from a high point in Ohio, Indiana, and Michigan as one goes further

[13] Munger, *American State Politics,* p. 207.

west or south in the region. In southern areas of the Middle
West, Democratic inclinations in rural areas contrast with
rural Republicanism in northern parts of the region. These
differences reflect the origin of early agricultural settlements:
those in the north were populated from anti-slavery Northeastern states or by German or Scandinavian immigrants, and
those of the south were settled by secession-inclined elements
from Maryland, Virginia, the Carolinas, Kentucky, and Tennessee. In Ohio, Indiana, and Illinois, Northern settlers came
overland and settled in the upper counties, while Southerners
came down the Ohio River and settled from the bottom upward. During the Civil War these two population groups represented the bases of sharp cleavage within the Middle West.
By now, their settlements and ideologies have become mixed
throughout Ohio, Indiana, and Illinois, but their disparate
origins continue to affect state policies. Because Democratic
parties have served both urban liberals and rural conservatives
while Republican parties have served both urban conservatives and rural liberals in Ohio, Indiana, and Illinois, each
party can provide an ideological home for present-day liberals
or conservatives. And partly because of the lack of sharp policy
differences between parties, the inter-party competition revolves about patronage jobs, personalities, and state contracts,
rather than issues of current policy.[14]

The Border States

The principal phenomenon described in John Fenton's
study of politics in the Border states of Maryland, West Virginia, Kentucky, and Missouri [15] is a competition between
three social-economic groups: Bourbons, Mountaineers, and a
combination of small farmers and urban workers. The Bourbons are descendants of settlers who came to rich agricultural
lands from former homes in the South Atlantic region. Although the Bourbons have dominated the Democratic party in
the Border states, they have long faced Republican opposition

14 Fenton, *Midwest Politics*, p. 225.
15 *Ibid.*

from the mountains, and intra-party opposition from liberally minded small farmers and urban workers. The Mountaineers —descended from original settlers who came to eastern Kentucky and southern Missouri from the highlands of western Virginia and North Carolina—were anti-secession during the Civil War and Republican after the war. Small farmers, urban organized labor, and urban Negroes have supported liberal factions within the Democratic party. Writing during the 1950's, Fenton perceived that the liberalism of politics in the North had already had an impact on politics in the Border states, and he predicted that his Border-state style of conflict would someday develop in the deeper South.

Alternate Views About the Transfer of Regional Traits

In contrast to Fenton's conception of North-Border-South regional change, there is another model of East-West regional drift. This is presented most clearly in Daniel J. Elazar's *American Federalism: A View from the States.*[16] He sees the transmission of political practices and norms following the migrations across the country from the seventeenth century onward. The states of the Middle West received one primary stream from the northern states of New England, New York, and Pennsylvania and another by way of the Ohio River from Maryland and Virginia. This second stream also helped to populate the Border states of western Maryland, West Virginia, Kentucky, and Missouri where its migrants mingled with others from the Carolinas. The western states of the South received their early settlers from Georgia and later from the dissatisfied residents of Alabama and Mississippi.

According to Elazar's model of migrating political forms, there is little reason to accept Fenton's prediction that the Border states of today resemble the South of tomorrow. Fenton argues that the South is "destined to copy" the Border states, but does not forecast the stimuli that will provoke the emulation. There is no prominent migratory stream from the Border states to the South; if there is any such stream at all, in fact,

16 New York: Thomas Y. Crowell, 1966.

it appears to go from the South to the Border states. But perhaps "moderate" Southerners emulate the Border states because they represent a more "advanced" model of politics without being so far advanced that they are out of the South's reach; or perhaps the intermediary character of the Border states reflects not so much an intermediary evolutionary stage as much as an intermediary position as recipients of initial settlers from both North and South.

Problems in the Regional Literature

A basic problem in the existing regional literature is that almost every piece deals with an individual region without making a serious effort to determine empirically how that region actually differs politically from other parts of the United States. A related problem is the employment of a single limited definition for each region: V. O. Key's classic study of Southern politics, for example, considers only the eleven states of the Confederacy; he makes no effort to test his findings in a larger conception of the South that includes Kentucky, Missouri, Oklahoma, West Virginia, Maryland, or Delaware. John Fenton's *Politics in the Border States* considers the politics of Missouri, Kentucky, West Virginia, and Maryland, but not Delaware or Oklahoma; his *Midwest Politics* examines Ohio, Indiana, Illinois, Michigan, Wisconsin, and Minnesota, but not Iowa, the Dakotas, Kansas, Nebraska, or Missouri. Unfortunately, no American region but New England is defined with sufficient clarity to permit an author to discuss regional politics without making some questionable assumptions about regional boundaries. The findings about one group of contiguous states may change as they are examined for a slightly larger or smaller conception of the region.

Because the regional literature has been content to describe politics in individual regions, it has made little headway toward the analysis of regional patterns. The implicit assumption in most writing is that the region at issue has certain unique features that reflect its own historic development. Yet without cross-regional comparisons, this conclusion is not acceptable. Even if certain areas are found to have distinctive political features, these may not be the products of specialized historical developments; the current style of politics, or the current level of public services, may reflect nothing more than the presence of certain social or economic characteristics in the region. If poverty shows a nationwide association with low voter turnout, for example, and voter turnout in the South is no lower than is predictable on the basis of poverty alone, then we should be reluctant to conclude that any special features of Southern culture—other than poverty—have produced its low scores on political participation.

Another shortcoming of the regional literature in political science is its narrow conception of the political process. The writings of V. O. Key, John H. Fenton, Duane Lockard, Thomas C. Donnelly, and Frank H. Jonas focus almost exclusively on electoral processes, party competition, and intraparty alignments. Political scientists have paid virtually no attention to regional peculiarities in governmental structure or public policies. By a regionally oriented examination of such topics as the nature of the legislature and executive, the level of government spending, tax systems, indebtedness, and federal-state-local relations, one may be able to perceive and understand more effectively the entire complex of regional political differences.

The Literature of Comparative State Politics

In its techniques of analysis this book bears a close resemblance to a second body of literature in political science: that which employs the American states as a laboratory for comparative research. Much of this work is related to the framework suggested by David Easton.[17] The work in comparative state politics employs hard data and sophisticated statistical techniques to examine relationships between "inputs" from the socioeconomic environment within each state, characteristics of the "state political system," and the "outputs" of policy

[17] *A Framework for Political Analysis* (Englewood Cliffs, N.J.: Prentice-Hall, 1965).

that are produced by the political and economic systems. This body of literature is relatively new, and begins with an article, published by Richard Dawson and James Robinson in 1963,[18] which set the pattern for one of the continuing controversies in the literature: do socioeconomic characteristics or political characteristics of the states exert the greater influence upon public policies?

Politics vs. Economics: A Major Dispute

Dawson and Robinson, Thomas R. Dye, and Richard I. Hofferbert have examined correlation coefficients among individual measures for policy outputs and the political traits of voter turnout, inter-party competition, the equity of legislative apportionment, and the socioeconomic characteristics of personal wealth, urbanization, industrialization, and education.[19] Finding that the strongest and statistically most important relationships occur between the policy outputs and the socioeconomic characteristics, they conclude that the nature of state political systems—at least on the dimensions of participation, competition and apportionment—has little influence on the nature of policies that is independent of social-economic influences on both politics and policy.

The early findings of the comparative state politics literature may have appeared threatening to political scientists; it looked as if features of the political system did not have a significant impact on the nature of public policies. In particular, this finding challenged the conclusions of several political scientists who had contributed to the regional literature. Key, Lockard, and Fenton, among others, had written that such factors as political participation, competition, and the equity of legislative apportionment had a great deal to do with the

18 Richard E. Dawson and James A. Robinson, "Interparty Competition, Economic Variables, and Welfare Politics in the American States," *Journal of Politics*, XXV (May 1963), 265–289.

19 See Thomas R. Dye, *Politics, Economics and the Public: Policy Outcomes in the American States* (Chicago: Rand McNally, 1966); and Richard I. Hofferbert, "Some Structural and Environmental Variables in the American States," *American Political Science Review*, LX (March 1966), 73–82.

nature of policies that states enacted and administered. However, the controversy about social-economic versus political determinants of policy has not ended. The literature of comparative state politics is constantly being enriched with new empirical findings. Clearly, there is much research left to be done before we attain a satisfactory understanding of the role that state politics plays in shaping the nature of public policies.

In an article that appeared after the early publications of comparative state literature, I employed a larger conception of "state politics" to demonstrate that certain political variables showed stronger relationships with policy measures than did any of several social-economic variables. In particular, the character of previous expenditure decisions and the proportion of spending responsibilities assigned to state (rather than local) governments have a profound impact on the current expenditures of state governments.[20] These findings demonstrate the importance of incremental budgeting among the political routines that precede policy decisions. And in a later piece, Hofferbert and I report the results of three separate factor analyses involving measures of state politics, state economics, and state policies.[21] The relationships among each state's scores on the resulting factors show that a political dimension labeled "turnout-competition" has a great deal to do with the nature of a service dimension labeled "welfare-education," independent of the effects of social-economic factors. This finding stands in direct contrast with the earlier work of Dawson and Robinson, Dye, and Hofferbert himself; it suggests that basic findings may rest upon the nature of the indicators and statistical techniques that are employed in the analysis, and it cautions restraint in the interpretation of any single item in this fast-growing body of political science.

[20] See my "Economic and Political Correlates of State Government Expenditures: General Tendencies and Deviant Cases," *Midwest Journal of Political Science,* XI (May 1967), 173–192; and *Spending in the American States* (Chicago: Rand McNally, 1968).

[21] Ira Sharkansky and Richard I. Hofferbert, "Dimensions of State Politics and Policy," *American Political Science Review,* LXIII (September 1969).

Problems in the Literature of Comparative State Politics

A close examination of what the current publications in the comparative state politics field do—and what they do not do—indicates that this fertile new field in political science has not yet been harvested fully. One shortcoming of the research that has been published to date is its emphasis on general findings that pertain to the collectivity of all the states. It may be generally true that certain features of party competition have no impact on state policies, but this does not mean that the nature of party alignments in any single state (or region) may not have great importance for policy decisions. In a single state, the nature of major-party leadership in the legislature, or the relationships between this leadership and the governor, may spell victory or defeat for the advocates of certain policy innovations, despite the fact that this would not show up in the studies that examine simplistic measures of "inter-party competition" at the macro-level of the fifty states.

Another limitation in the research in comparative state politics lies in the excessive reliance on expenditure figures as measures of policy "outputs." Some research has found that the relationships between spending and other types of policy or service measures are, at best, tenuous.[22] For this reason, it is risky to conclude that findings based upon the analysis of government expenditures also have meaning for other characteristics of state policy.

At the same time that the studies of comparative state politics have relied upon simplistic measures of expenditure as policy surrogates, they have also failed to examine the distribution of policy benefits among various social and economic segments of the state population. The focus has been upon the total level of "outputs" (usually measured by expenditures) produced by a state, instead of upon the nature of outputs given to the members of each social or economic group within the state.

Finally, the research in comparative state politics has generally overlooked the possibilities inherent in time-series anal-

22 See my "Government Expenditures and Public Services in the American States," *American Political Science Review*, LXI (December 1967), 1066–1077.

ysis. Most of the findings pertain only to the period encompassed by the 1960–1962 *Census of Population* and/or *Census of Governments*. It is possible that findings relevant to this era have some lasting meaning for our understanding of American politics, but this may not be the case. Indeed, two of Hofferbert's papers testify to the wide variations in economic-political relationships that may occur between two time periods.[23] Characteristics of a historical era may have a great deal to do with the dependence of politicians on economic resources within their jurisdiction, or with their responsiveness to particular social or economic groups. It is shortsighted to undertake a major analysis without some concern for changes in systemic relationships over time, and it is misleading to report the findings of such research without a strong caveat about the historical condition.

As noted in Chapter 1, this book attempts to remedy some of the problems in the literatures of regional political science and of comparative state politics. It adds to the regional literature by examining regions across the country, by considering alternate definitions of each region, by considering a wide range of indicators for both state politics and policy, and by testing the regional findings for the influence of current economic conditions. It adds to the literature on comparative state politics by adding the nominal variable of "region" to the statistical analysis of politics and policy, by looking at changes in regional patterns over time, and by suggesting historical, cultural, or political explanations for these regional patterns that are not amenable to explanation by current economic conditions.

[23] See his "Stability and Change in Some Social Correlates of Political Participation and Policy Outputs in the States," unpublished paper delivered at the Annual Meeting of the Southwestern Social Science Association, 1967; and "Composition and Political Relevance of Major Socioeconomic Dimensions of the American States: 1890–1960," *Midwest Journal of Political Science*, XII (1968).

APPENDIX B

SOURCES OF VARIABLES

The variables listed in this Appendix are shown in the order with which they are presented in Chapter 2. They are the measures which assess regional traits in state politics and public policy. Many of the variables are not found in the following sources in the same form in which they are analyzed. To fit the purposes of this book, it has been necessary to combine several "raw" measures in order to correct for population size or other "control" variables. This Appendix notes the source for each variable. If a reader wishes to replicate part of this study, or use similar variables in order to pursue additional analysis, it will be necessary to note carefully the variables as they are described in Chapter 2, so that appropriate corrections of the raw data may be made. Unless it is noted otherwise, the publications listed below come from the U.S. Government Printing Office in Washington, D.C.

VARIABLE	SOURCE
1) U.S. Representative turnout	*Statistical Abstract, 1964*
2) turnout for governor	*Ibid.*
3) lower house competition	*Ibid.*
4) upper house competition	*Ibid.*
5) U.S. Representative competition	*Ibid.*
6) governor competition	*Ibid.*
7) governor tenure	*Ibid.*
8) lower house tenure	*Ibid.*
9) upper house tenure	*Ibid.*
10) Schubert-Press apportionment index	*American Political Science Review,* LVIII (1964), 969
11) Dauer-Kelsay apportionment index	Paul T. David and Ralph Eisenberg, *Devaluation of the Urban and Suburban Vote* (Charlottesville: Bureau of Public Administration University of Virginia, 1961), p. 5
12) David-Eisenberg apportionment index	*Ibid.,* p. 15
13) number of legislators	*Statistical Abstract, 1964*
14) government employees	*Ibid.*
15) number of bills introduced	*Book of the States, 1964–1965* (Chicago: Council of State Governments, 1964)
16) number of bills passed	*Ibid.*
17) length of legislative session	*Ibid.*
18) legislators' compensation	*Ibid.*
19) government employees' salary	*Statistical Abstract, 1964*
20) merit system coverage	*Book of the States, 1964–1965*
21) total state expenditures/capita	*Compendium of State Government Finances, 1962*
22) state education expenditures/ capita	*Ibid.*
23) state highway expenditures/ capita	*Ibid.*
24) state welfare expenditures/ capita	*Ibid.*

VARIABLE	SOURCE
25) total state + local expend/capita	*Compendium of Government Finances* (Census of Governments, 1962)
26) state + local educ. expend/ capita	*Ibid.*
27) state + local highw. expend/ capita	*Ibid.*
28) state + local welfare expend/ capita	*Ibid.*
29) state tax effort	*Compendium of State Government Finances, 1962*
30) state and local tax effort	*Compendium of Government Finances* (Census of Governments, 1962)
31) property tax revenues/capita	*Ibid.*
32) general sales tax revenues/capita	*Ibid.*
33) excise tax revenues/capita	*Ibid.*
34) motor-vehicle tax revenues/ capita	*Ibid.*
35) income tax revenues/capita	*Ibid.*
36) current charges/capita	*Ibid.*
37) debt/capita	*Ibid.*
38) state + local revenue allocated to state	*Ibid.*
39) state + local revenue from non-local sources	*Ibid.*
40) state revenue coming from federal government	*Compendium of State Government Finances, 1962*
41) state and local revenue from federal government	*Compendium of Government Finances* (Census of Governments, 1962)
42) participation in school lunch program	*Statistical Abstract, 1964*
43) participation in vocational education	*Ibid.*
44) persons in process of vocational rehabilitation	*Ibid.*

VARIABLE	SOURCE
45) persons completing vocational rehabilitation	*Ibid.*
46) incidence of high-school graduations	*Rankings of the States* (National Education Association, 1963)
47) incidence of success in mental exam	*Ibid.*
48) total road mileage/capita	*Book of the States, 1964–1965*
49) rural mileage/rural resident	*Statistical Abstract, 1964*
50) urban mileage/urban resident	*Ibid.*
51) percentage Interstate completed	*Ibid.*
52) percentage of farms on paved roads	*Census of Agriculture, 1959*
53) residents/motor-vehicle death	*Statistical Abstract, 1964*
54) average payment, AFDC	*Ibid.*
55) average payment, OAA	*Ibid.*
56) average payment, AB	*Ibid.*
57) average payment, APTD	*Ibid.*
58) incidence of recipients, AFDC	*Ibid.*
59) incidence of recipients, OAA	*Ibid.*
60) incidence of recipients, AB	*Ibid.*
61) incidence of recipients, APTD	*Ibid.*

INDEX